CATCH & RELEASE:

How to Spot a Throwback

~Your Guide to Raising the Bar When Dating~

Rachel Fiori & Melissa Fiori

M⊙tivational PRESS®

LEADERS IN GLOBAL PUBLISHING

Published by Motivational Press, Inc.
1777 Aurora Road
Melbourne, Florida, 32935
www.MotivationalPress.com

Copyright 2018 © by Rachel Fiori & Melissa Fiori
Illustrations by Jerry Kong

Manufactured in the United States of America.

ISBN: 978-1-62865-555-1

Contents

ACKNOWLEDGEMENTS

We sisters would like to extend our love and appreciation to all of our friends and family who supported us on this fishing expedition. Your laughter at our fish tales and encouragement to not cut the line before this book got published means the world to us.

SPECIAL THANKS

Joyce H. Yohe & Paul K. Yohe, II

Maria Bufalino • Valerie Cannavo

Tina Christodouleas-Tabakoviç • Greg DuMond • Erin Dumond

Chad Emerich • Christina Giunta • Edwin Gomez

Krystal Hawkins-Chavez • Jenn Kandl

Jennifer Kennedy • Deborah Klein • Jerry Kong

Tammy Pilat Magiera • Thomas Martinelli Jr.

Sameer K. Mathur • Amy McCann • Tim Miller

• Bianca Rodriguez• Ryan Schofield • Jackie & Ken Yohe

Michelle Zerpa • Omar Zohur

NOTE TO THE READER

While the fish tales in this book were inspired by actual events, all identities have been changed to preserve anonymity (except for the Big Tuna). The chapter titles were inspired by actual fish names (some of the names were too funny to pass up!) and we've made a *modest* attempt to link the natural fish behavior to human male behavior. In some instances they do overlap, in other instances they don't at all.

In any case—our apologies to the fish!

INTRODUCTION

IT ALL STARTED ONE NIGHT after Rachel got home from a "you-will-NOT-believe what-just-happened-to-me" date and called her sister to tell the unbelievable tale. As Rachel exclaimed, "I couldn't make this stuff up if I wanted to", Melissa casually stated, "yeah, we should write a book." Then, Bam! Like a fish jumping out of water the ideas started flowing about all the different types of *THROW BACKS* there are and we started relating each different type of man to various types of fish. We doubled over with laughter as we compared fish to men! Even after the conversation ended our heads were churning with examples, stories and scenarios. Then, voila! This book was born.

We decided we wanted to not only share our outlandish stories, but also to use this as a platform to end the bad relationship cycles that so many men and women of all ages experience. We hoped other women would laugh as hard as we had, that they could relate and, most importantly, that they'd be inspired to take action when it comes to *THROW BACKS*. We hoped men would enjoy it too and would change their ways if they realized they were one of the *THROW BACKS*. We intended that the book would send a positive message about scoring HEALTHY relationships, because truth be told—we're all really looking for a great **catch**! We're looking for that special someone, the one who will love us when we're at our best <u>and</u> our worst, someone who we can laugh and cry with, someone to grow old with, someone to spend our days and nights with, someone with whom to share the mundane and the extraordinary. We want someone who is respectful, considerate, has integrity, speaks our love language, someone who makes us a priority, and really appreciates us for who we are.

In order to find all of that, we've got to get GRITTY. Yes, IF we are to find someone who we sincerely like and enjoy spending time with, someone who respects us for who we are and what we are, and someone we respect in return, we have to be brave. If we are to find someone with whom we feel safe, happy, at peace and *at home*, we have to be courageous. What does this require? It requires that we **take a hard look at ourselves, our values, our standards, our behaviors, and our choices**.

If you don't yet know who you are, then you have no business fishing. Put down the pole and steer clear of the shore, bank, dock or stream! Until you know yourself and have worked on yourself enough to be a healthy person who doesn't *need* a partner to make you happy, then all of your **catches** will be washed up. If you do know yourself and look at having a partner as a compliment in your life and not a necessity, then you can reap the benefits of what a healthy and fulfilling relationship can bring.

Not knowing and growing yourself is a recipe for disaster. When we look outside of ourselves, we lower our standards as to what is acceptable behavior for us and from the opposite sex. We settle for bad behavior and even make excuses for it.

Ladies, we've lowered the bar so much that guys don't have to demonstrate QUALITY in order to win our affections, AND we seem to have developed a neglect for listening to and trusting our instincts. We downplay disrespectful behaviors when our intuition tells us not to! I mean, *what in the world happens to a woman's intuition when there's a penis in the room?* A million and one red-flags could be slapping us in the face, telling us this guy is bad news and utterly *terrible* for us and we just throw on a really good push-up bra, put our blinders on, flip our hair, lower our standards, and pretend that everything is ok. Stop pretending!! Take the damn blinders off and remove those chicken cutlets from your bra! So many women ignore their instincts and foolishly accept guys' outlandish and disrespectful behaviors because mainstream society deems it acceptable for men to act like pigs and for women to just live with it. We are so sick of this standard and even more disgusted by our fellow sisters who continually lower their guidelines for what a good **catch** really is. Many women's actions send the message that guys can treat them like crap, or just simply 'be around' and that's good enough for the guy to receive loyalty, trust, and companionship from a woman. Then these very same women turn around and whine and cry about the way their man treats them. Hey ladies, these guys are *THROW BACKS*!! If you want the cream-of-the-crop, or to find a great **catch**, then **STOP SETTLING!!!!!**

Let's not forget the guys. Gentlemen, you deserve to have that special **catch** as well, but you ALSO need to dig deep within and know what you truly value in a partnership. Instead of demeaning yourself by succumbing to the stereotypical "male behaviors," raise your own personal standards in order to find true happiness. Everyone must understand a partnership takes effort and commitment, and you must know yourself before someone else joins you on your journey. Guys, c'mon! You MUST know that so much of the provocative behavior that happens in clubs is a reflection of low self-esteem that both you and women have of themselves. Without self-worth many men and women seek validation and meeting the need of significance through sexual prowess. Women will openly flirt with taken men, and/or approach boyfriends in both the absence AND presence of the girlfriend—while making their way to a *number* of other guys in the bar. You must know how little a person in that "condition" has to offer you. If you take advantage of that, if you capitalize on their insecurities, naïveté, and "advertising," what does that say about YOU, YOUR VALUES, YOUR CHARACTER, and who YOU ARE as a person? It just shows that you're a user and have very low standards for yourself. And maintaining low standards is always a relfection of how you actually feel about yourself, despite what you try to show to the world.

EVERYONE needs to know that YOU DON'T GET WHAT YOU WANT IN LIFE, YOU GET WHAT YOU ARE.

Therefore, if you're an inconsiderate, selfish, materialistic, insecure, ego-driven, megalomaniac (ie, a person characterized by delusional fantasies of wealth, power, grandeur, and omnipotence) you will attract others with the same disposition into your life. On the other hand, if you're selfless and kind, compassionate, considerate, generous, self-assured, and the like, the megalomaniacs won't even be interested in you. Accordingly, you've opened the door to dating higher quality people versus dating THROW BACKS·

So, why is it so tough to find a REALLY good **catch**? It's our own damn, collective fault!!! It is our fault for lowering the bar, for allowing standards to diminish, for ignoring our instincts, for not knowing ourselves, and most importantly for NOT CHANGING AND GROWING into the most magnificent versions of ourselves before settling down. So, while each of us engages in some deep self-reflection, assesses our value system, and examines the choices and behavioral patterns we make in life, this book is here to help. While we strip away the labels and nonsense about who we are and discover our deeper, more authentic selves, while we figure out what we want to do/achieve/experience this book is your guide. You are being nudged to get clear, to learn how to set healthy boundaries, and to change within yourself what you no longer want to experience in your relationships.

This book is your guide to raising the bar when dating… It helps you spot undesirables through guidance, lessons and real life stories so you can THROW BACK the losers and reel in your **catch**. Ladies, your ultimate **catch** is the **BIG TUNA**. Gentlemen, yours is the **ANGEL FISH**. Now, there is no *one size fits all* when it comes to the **Big Tuna** or the **Angel Fish**. We're all looking for that person who's our best fit! We're each searching for a partner who shares the same values, who shares a related set of guiding principles. Someone who has parallel moral and ethical standards, has compatible ideals, and is headed in a similar direction. What might be a **catch** for <u>you</u> might not be a **catch** for <u>someone else.</u>

What's the best way to find your **Big Tuna / Angel Fish**? Ladies, truly know yourself, trust your instincts and STOP SETTLING! Guys, figure out what you truly value, don't be controlled by your ego, stop using female *THROW BACKS* for your own sexual gratification, and be sure you're not one of the *THROW BACKS*.

It might seem like the only thing out there is a bunch of pond scum, but we're here to say that YES! there are **Big Tunas** and **Angel Fish** out there! However, throughout the journey, to swim to the ultimate **catch**, most people have to sort through a number of undesirables before reeling in that special someone. Dating *THROW BACKS* will slow down your quest for that one, extraordinary **catch** .... So read on to learn about the many types of *THROW BACKS* to be on alert for because they delay you (and can prevent you) from finding your ultimate **catch**.

Why should you *really* read this book?

First, to knock some COMMON SENSE back into you! The bad behaviors we call attention to are just that – BAD BEHAVIORS! They are dysfunctional, selfish, unloving ways of behaving when dating or when in a relationship with someone. If you're with someone who behaves like any one of the *THROW BACKS* profiled in this book, COMMON SENSE tells you to throw that fish back! Also, it is only common sense that if *you* exhibit the behaviors outlined in this material, then you're not in a position to be in a relationship. If YOU don't know YOU, (including the good, the bad, and the ugly) and if you're not willing to work on and change YOU, then how can you expect someone ELSE to treat you with the digninity, respect, loyalty and love that you wish you had?

Secondly, because these stories are REAL. They are based off of true stories that were screaming to be told. We've dated, were college and graduate students, and are professionals. Scores of University students have passed through Melissa's office in search of advice, and countless people have sought out life and relationship coaching with Rachel. Thus, the viewpoints we share are from life's lessons, from professional training and expertise, and from seeking out continuous knowledge and training as professionals.

Thirdly, because we've got a POSITIVE message of self-awareness, empowerment, and growth while sprinkling in some hilarious stories about terrible behavior. We definitely poke fun at *THROW BACKS,* but we ultimately hold women accountable for taking the reins of their own lives, and for being responsible for their own choices.

Enjoy these fish tales! Hopefully this book will help you to regain your sense of dignity when in relationships, to increase your confidence and personal power, and to make better choices when it comes to love. If you don't start raising the bar for yourself and for those you choose to date, then you'll continue to run in the hamster wheel of bad relationships. No one truly wants that. So get comfortable, prepare to take a long, hard look at yourself, and let the game of "no more *THROW BACKS*" begin!

Enjoy!

THROW BACKS

PIRANHA

THE FRAT BOY. . .

Generally speaking, at a young age males are typically considered harmless and docile until they're initiated into a fraternity. With the group mentality of older, more skilled *PIRANHA* to learn from, the younger males quickly learn how to hunt and score chicks. They become armed and dangerous with a group mentality and a ferocious sexual appetite. They don't pay attention to "standards" like intelligence, independence, and diligence. No!! They will feast on almost anyone who's willing to give them what they want. In fact, intellect, autonomy, and conscientiousness are qualities that *PIRANHAS* characteristically shy away from because women who hold those standards command respect.

PIRANHAS have the ability to attack with such cunningness that they can quickly strip a woman of her reputation and dignity in a matter of hours or even minutes! The infamous "walk-of-shame," often seals the deal on the female victim's self and external respect, as she scurries home after a night of sexual exploration with one of the *PIRANHAS* that preyed on her.

Unfortunately, there continues to be an appalling double standard when it comes to male vs. female reputations. Males are saluted for sleeping around, while females are labeled negatively for engaging in even minor sexual activity. *PIRANHAS* tend to keep track of girls they deem as "easy" and will strategize ways for other *PIRANHAS* to benefit from these girls' promiscuity. Although it may seem like harmless fun at the time, and that everyone does it, there are certain extreme behaviors that do not need to be displayed just to get some pathetic horny guy's attention.

I have male college friends that even after almost ten years post-graduation, still reminisce about what girl performed what sexual act on what "brothers." I even hear guys time and time again pat themselves on the back about getting a blowjob from a girl in the backseat of a car in high school. *High school!* This guy was telling a story from over twenty years ago like it was yesterday! Like somehow that story defines him as a real man! Remember this, ladies, the things a female does even at a very young age, always find a way to stick around. Unfortunately no matter how much she wants it to be forgotten, somehow it never is.

Women— you deserve to have fun too!! Just be smarter about it. Use your brains instead of your body and take control of situations instead of handing the control over on a silver platter to any guy that seems to give you attention.

PIRANHAS aren't limited to college age. They can be of any age. The thing to remember is that their distasteful behaviors are magnified in groups. They encourage each other to behave in scumbag ways to the point of turning a previously decent man into a hunter of prey. The group mentality promotes bad behaviors and discourages respectful, loving attitudes towards women.

One Saturday morning I was on my way to the library when I passed Sara. She had spent the night with her boyfriend after his fraternity had a party that ran from dusk 'till dawn. We said hello in passing – she needed to get home to shower and have breakfast and I needed to get to the library, but right after our paths crossed, some neighboring frat boys began to chant "Walk of shame! Walk of shame!" At Sara. WTF?! Not only had Sara and Brent been dating for years, those guys weren't spewing their double standards at any of the "gentlemen" making their way home from their girlfriends' (or trists!) from the night before!

Is your dude a *PIRANHA*?

☐ Does he kiss and tell?

☐ Does he hook up with *any* girl?

☐ Does he call your fling a walk of shame, but label himself a mac daddy?

☐ Is he heavily influenced by his *PIRANHA* brothers and behave differently when he's with the group vs. when alone with you?

☐ Will he lie to cover his tail fin?

☐ Has he sent you an unsolicited dick pic?

If you've spotted a *PIRANHA*, get back in the boat! Speed away! Leave him in the treacherous waters and make your way to safety without delay! Let some other beginner earn herself a bad reputation or a spot on a fraternity *"wall of shame,"* while you paddle your way towards the 'toy' store!

BARRACUDA

"LIE-IN-WAIT...THEN YOU'RE MINE"

WHEN IT COMES TO THE **BARRACUDAS** physical appearance, they are not necessarily your typical "jock" type. While many are very good looking, they might also be the guy you overlook the first time you scan a room. Or they might be "the nice guy" of the group or the slightly less attractive guy who doesn't always "get the girl". They interact socially, both singly and in schools.

However, don't be fooled - **BARRACUDAS** are voracious predators and are known for herding multiple fish into shallow waters and then guarding over them until they are ready for another meal. They hunt using a classic example of *lie-in-wait*. Often they prey on girls who are suffering from heartbreak or a breakup, who are vulnerable and in need of feeling attractive and wanted by the opposite sex. **BARRACUDAS** tend to befriend all types of girls, many of whom are in relationships. They can be just one of your guy friends, or might be one of your boyfriend's friends, who is always around and seems to be really nice. They establish themselves as harmless and then use the *lie-in-wait* tactic for your relationship to end. They are cunning and know they stand a much better chance of reeling you in once you are in a penetrable emotional state, where your defenses are down, and they can be viewed as the great guy who somehow rescued you.

If your relationship has just ended and you are approached by either one of your ex's friends or one of your guy friends and they say something along the lines of, "I've liked you all along, but didn't make a move because I respected your relationship." Then a red flag should go up! You have no way of knowing how many other girls he's attempted to ambush and there is no guarantee he is not saying the same things to other girls simultaneously. Remember the *BARRACUDA* has a way to keep many opportunities around him at all times.

TRAY

I met Andy and a group of his friends one night while out with a girlfriend from work. Andy and I hit it off and began spending a lot of time getting to know each other. Andy was a tall 6'4", muscular, funny, sexy, sweet heart of a guy, who was never shy about showering me with compliments. He definitely showed **Big Tuna** potential! His friends Neal and Tray, whom I often spent time with as well, were hilarious and fun to be around. One night Andy, Neal and I had plans to go out. Since Tray wasn't with us that night the others took the opportunity to "warn" me about Tray. They told me several stories of how Tray seemed to wait around for Neal or Andy to break up with a girlfriend and then suddenly pour his heart out to her exclaiming he had always wanted to be with her, but kept his distance out of respect for his friend and their relationship. Having that insight about Tray definitely made me see him in a different light. I saw the very subtle signs of him closing in on girls that Neal approached first. When paid close attention to, I could see the cunningness of Tray's strategies and that he was indeed a very skilled **BARRACUDA**.

PORTER & MARISSA

Marissa could hear the music of her favorite cd playing when she got to the front door. When she opened it the lights were low and the table had been beautifully set for two. Deliciously savory aromas wafted from the kitchen. There was a bouquet of red roses and a trail of petals marking the way to the table and encircling the bottle of chilled champagne that was placed in the center. Porter was standing there with a poem in hand – Marissa's favorite poem of all time – and he began to recite it. After he read the poem he toasted to her health, and all the years they would spend together, in light of the results of her recent tests with the doctors coming back as cancer-free.

Sounds like the actions of BIG TUNA– except – IT NEVER HAPPENED. Porter performed that scenario for an acting class he was taking. Everyone praised his performance and told him how great he was as they wiped the tears from their eyes. Porter left satisfied with himself, this Barracuda was hunting and using lie-in-wait tactics. He was basically setting himself up to be thought of as the great boyfriend, the sensitive caring guy that all the ladies in the class wish they had. That way if/when things went south with the ungrateful Marissa, he would have established how wonderful, thoughtful, caring, considerate, and awesome he is for the single - and soon to be single ladies- to recall and act upon.

Here's what really happened, it was Marissa's second round of treatments. The year before they had removed suspicious tissue, but they thought they got it all. When she went in for her check-up, she was not expecting them to report that she would have to schedule an additional procedure. The procedure was scheduled for three weeks later and when that day arrived, Porter had no idea it was on that day because he never logged it on his calendar. Marissa had expected him to go with her, not only for the emotional support, but also because she would be sore and shouldn't drive after the procedure. Porter wasn't holding a job that tied him to an office, he had no time clock to punch, and he had money coming in from a family member. He could have taken off work, but he didn't. He told Marissa he was under pressure, that every workday mattered, and how, if he went with her, he would be missing a full day of work.

So, Marissa let him off the hook. "Ok, that's fine. I need your support, but if you're just going to be obsessing the whole time, then you're just going to stress me before the procedure. Stay back and get your work done, just be here this evening to be with me when I get home."

Porter did just the opposite. The man who emphasized the importance of work and meeting his quotas, spent the afternoon getting high. Marissa had to wait in the office for an hour before the nausea subsided to the point that she could drive herself home, queasy and sore, only to discover that Porter spent the day smoking. Just to add insult to injury, shortly after she collapsed on the couch, he announced that he was going to pop into a different acting class that he hadn't visited for nearly five weeks.

He was shrewd, sly and MANIPULATIVE!! The swooning women in that room had no reason to believe that Porter was the opposite. In Porter's made up scenario he paints himself as the "nice guy," and gets all the women in the class to start thinking of him in a different way, allowing him to keep many opportunities around him at all times — *You see ladies... this is how I'd treat you if you were mine. When this woman leaves me for neglecting her, I've set up a scenario in which you'll come to me when your boyfriend lets you down and we'll get away with it because we're "friends from class"... Better yet, if I'm single when that happens, I've already fooled you into thinking I'm actually the guy from my made up scene.*

How does a person know if they reeled in a Barracuda? Marissa says that in retrospect, the warning signs were there. About nine months before the story above took place; Marissa had had to go in for a major surgery. While Porter did have the date on his calendar for this one, and did drive her to and from the hospital, he went on about how busy he was and how much he had on his plate. Before the surgery, he was glued to his cell phone, sending texts and navigating social media, to the point he gave no attention to the procedures.

Marissa had asked him to stay at the surgical center the entire time, and told him they'd allow him back to be with her immediately before and then immediately after the surgery. She told him she was scared and she was grateful that he'd be there to help her get through. So, they took her back and prepped her, but when the nurses went out to find Porter, he was gone. He took off. He left the surgical center to "run some errands." Why not? What Marissa doesn't know won't hurt her, right? Besides, he didn't *know they were going to bring him back before the* surgery, (how could he when he was glued to his phone?!) He was just so busy, too busy, apparently, to pay attention to what he was asked, to pay attention to the procedures, to acquiesce to a heart-felt request from a woman about to go into a scary surgery, or to care about anything other than his own needs. When he did show up he charmed the nurses with his good-guy story about how he just stepped out and thought he had time to get back, and blah, blah, blah. They bought it and sang his praises. While they chattered on about how sweet Porter was, about how concerned he was, and how smitten he was with Marissa, she smiled outwardly, but questioned it inside. *If all that were true, why did he leave? Why wasn't he here? I told him I needed him by my side. I explicitly asked for it, yet he took off anyway. Everyone else is brushing this off. Am I over reacting or is this a red flag?*

Porter's **BARRACUDA** tendencies manifest themselves in other ways as well. When Marissa wanted to go out for drinks, go to dinner, try new bars or go to new places, Porter would refuse.

"You know I can't afford that and you know I don't have the time. I'm trying to build my career."

Yet, as soon as it was *someone else's birthday*, or as soon as friends wanted to meet up or go out, Porter somehow had the time and the money!

—End the workday around five or six so Marissa and Porter could spend some quality time together? What a ludicrous request on Marissa's part. She CLEARLY was very unsympathetic to Porter's situation. End the workday at five or six when Marissa isn't around – absolutely!

—Eat out? Not possible when it came to Marissa, but if one of his business partners or friends wanted to grab lunch, dinner, or drinks there was no stopping him! He suddenly had all the time and money in the world!

—Go out? *Unless you've got the money to pay for it, Marissa, you know I've got bills to pay.* Go with friends?! Hell yeah! *I mean, it was boring Marissa who kept me from all of this!*

There he was, again, painting himself as the "nice guy," dating this terrible woman who never wanted to do anything. Only, the reality was the opposite – she was DYING to go out and have fun. But, a *BARRACUDA* can't be a *BARRACUDA* with his girlfriend around… so, he made sure he was always in a situation where he could paint himself the way he wanted to be seen.

Pay attention! Listen to your instincts. If something is nagging at you inside, take note. That uncomfortable feeling Marissa had inside is because although Porter had the appearances of a catch, she really had a *BARRACUDA* on the line!

BARRACUDAS are:

☐ Vicious (although seemingly docile)—they'll say the right things at the right time.

☐ Conniving – they exercise patience and know when to make their move.

☐ Observant—they carefully watch everyone's scene so they can tailor their approach to each person's individual weak spots.

☐ Masters – at lie-in-wait tactics.

☐ PHONY – They make themselves out to be harmless good guys, with no agenda.

☐ SCHEMING – they take it all in and build a strategy for getting what they want.

DOG FISH

THE STEREOTYPICAL "MEN ARE DOGS" GUY

THESE FISH ARE EVERYWHERE and can be difficult to swim away from. As soon as you're able to break free it seems as though you're swimming straight toward another *DOG FISH*. It"s frustrating to be dealing constantly with a guy who can't quite look you in the eyes because he can't take them off your body. What's worse is he can't seem to take them off of other girls' bodies either! However, it doesn't stop there. Their behaviors can run from milder to more extreme, but their choices are always true to their reputation: these fish are *DOGS*. They'll say anything to get what they want, will bend the truth and lie outrightly to get their desires met, they'll manipulate and control every situation to guarantee their wanted outcome. They will suppress information flow or dance around answering simple questions, lie by omission, and will do all of this with an attitude of righteousness.

If you're hanging out with a guy who's more interested in your curves than your ideas … or thinks your eyes have somehow migrated to your chest, then it's pretty clear that you're with a *DOG FISH*!

ANGELO

Angelo and I met when we were in our early twenties. We were both working on degrees and met through a mutual friend. We ended up dating for a short while. We hit it off well and got along glowingly, but we knew from the beginning that there was no future. Not only were we very young, but also we were both about to go abroad to different countries and really didn't know where that would take either one of us. We parted as friends and managed to stay in touch over the years.

Eight years later we found ourselves in touch again—both of us single. We decided to get together for a weekend. When we got together it was if no time had passed. We still got along great and there was still a dynamic…BUT… he had turned into such a *DOG FISH*!

We had a weekend getaway where we met up with a grad-school buddy of his. We had a pleasant time trekking around the city and hanging out with the friend and his girlfriend.

Well, that evening we decided to go out for drinks and to a hot-spot for salsa dancing. The girlfriend invited one of her friends along and we hit the town.

That invite unleashed the hound. Our "romantic" weekend, turned into Angelo courting the friend's friend and trying to initiate a threesome. What's even worse is the man who exhibited this behavior was annoyed when he viewed pictures from that evening, revealing that someone had put their hand on my ass—and it wasn't him! "No honor among theives," he murmured, "he's such a dog."

I should have known, this guy had just broken up with a long term girlfriend whom he claimed to want to marry. Yes, he claimed to want to marry her, but told me stories of liaisons and trists with other women in his "future-wife's" absence.

It goes without saying that he was a *THROW BACK!* While his book-smart intelligence quota was Ivy League, his emotional IQ didn't even register on the charts!

CHRISTIAN

Christian wasn't that much different. We met at a conference and discovered we had a friend in common and hit it off instantly.

We spent a lot of time together. He liked to talk and was an interesting guy. He was very smart and had a lot of stories to tell, so I enjoyed myself. Plus, since he had a girlfriend, I saw him as no threat and our time together as innocent.

There was a physical attraction underlying the intellectual attraction, but I just thought that to be the icing on the platonic cake. For me, it was a bonus because I had been on many a dry fishing expedition and was just enjoying a no-pressure situation. It took me most of the week before I realized it might not be so innocent from his side. He was on the prowl and had me in his sights. Everyone else could see it and they labeled us as the "Conference Couple;" people approached me telling me what a cute couple we were, to which I replied we were only friends.

And we were…until the last night. He walked me back to my room, but on this night he planted a kiss. I gave in for a second and then put a stop to it, after all he had a girlfriend.

The next morning I called to say final goodbyes to everyone and I NEVER should have done so. His goodbye lead to a kiss and a lot of temptation. It had been so long since anyone had held my hand or cuddled with me, let alone had kissed me, and I was hurting for a little affection. But at the price of being "that woman?!" I thought not.

"Don't you have a girlfriend?" I asked him.

"It's complicated," he replied.

"Yeah, of course it's complicated; it *would* be complicated if you behave this way when she is out of sight," I thought.

And that was that, we went our separate ways and things didn't go any further. Thank God because it turns out that Christian's "girlfriend" was actually his *wife* and they decided to work things out. I hope he's able to keep his fish in his pants and his tentacles to himself.

Daryl & Evan

Daryl and Evan were friends of mine from high-school. I ran into Daryl by chance one day, when I stopped to treat myself to a latté. We hadn't seen each other in quite a few years and had a lot of catching up to do, and luckily another high-school friend, Evan, was going to be in town in just a few days. We decided to meet up for dinner and drinks.

We started off having a blast—catching up on who was where and who was doing what. We updated each other pretty thoroughly and then began speaking about high-school. Hearing some of the infamous stories retold was quite a laugh. It is clear our reasoning area of the brain does not develop until our mid twenties or else we'd not make such stupid choices as teens!! Speaking of stupid choices… the conversation turned to sex, conquests and relationships of yore. Some of the stories I hadn't heard before, (lucky me!) while some were just as funny as the first time I heard them. What was not so funny is the conversation took a turn to the present when they tried to convince me to have a threesome with them after dinner.

Now, both of these guys were married men! Daryl had been married for quite a few years to a very successful career-woman and Evan was married and had a son! Yet—there they were, quite seriously trying to get me to go to bed with them. I first tried to shake the conversation, change the subject, divert our attention, but to no avail. Finally, when I had had enough, I looked Evan straight in the eyes and said to him,

"If you can go home and look your child in the eyes and tell him you disrespected him, his mother, and your marriage… If you can go home and look him in the eyes and tell him that a lay was more important than his right to grow up in an unbroken home… that your need for a fling took priority over his needs and everything else… I'll do it. Now, I'm going to excuse myself and when I get back from the bathroom I assume you'll be able to tell me if you can do that or not."

Once I returned from the bathroom the topic of conversation changed drastically, but I ended the night very quickly after that. I chose not to continue to be in the company of men who are disrespectful. That's what setting boundaries is all about. Once you realize a person's true intentions, and those intentions are negative, disrespectful or demeaning, you have NO reason to continue to spend time with that person.

Keith

Keith and Damian are two guys I went to college with. They were roommates in a fraternity and very close friends. I used to hang out with these guys fairly frequently and always had a good time. Interestingly Keith was dating a girl, Emma, who lived across the hall from me in the dorms. Damian had a girlfriend back home as well as one at college.

Keith called me one day to invite me and a group of friends to hang out that night. So I went up to Keith's fraternity to hang out with him, his roommate, and several others. Suddenly there was a knock on the door and a drunken female voice called out, *"Keith, are you in there?"* It was Emma! Keith immediately covered my mouth with his hand and put his finger to his lips and gestured, *Sshhh*! I looked at him startled. His roommate called to Emma through the door and told her Keith wasn't there, but he'd have him call her later.

Meanwhile, Keith was pulling me up from the couch and shoving me up the ladder into his top bunk. We both got to the top bunk, covered up with a blanket, and Keith told me not to make a sound. I whispered to him, "*What the hell is going on?*" And he replied, "*Remember when I told you that Emma and I were broken up? Well, we're not exactly broken up and I'm not supposed to hang out with you. . . well, ever*".

Ummmm, *what?*!?!? This information would have been pretty important to know before 1) I accepted the invite to their party and 2) Emma decided to spontaneously show up at the door!

It turns out they hadn't broken up, he just told me that so I would hang out with him. Since Emma apparently already thought that he was cheating on her with *me*, she made him promise he wouldn't hang out with me ever again. Once more— information that would have been pertinent before the evening began.

Emma refused to leave until someone opened the door and she could see for herself that Keith wasn't there because she *swore she heard his voice!* Damian finally let her in and she ended up hanging out for about fifteen minutes before she announced she had to go to the bathroom. Yes, Keith and I were still hiding quietly under the blankets on the top bunk, with Emma about five feet below us. Once Emma left the room and entered the bathroom, Keith shoved me out of bed, and one of his friends grabbed my hand and said, "*Quick, follow me!*"

The next thing I knew we were all racing down the hall to go hide in this guy's room. After waiting until the coast was clear, I was snuck out of the fraternity by a back entrance and walked to my dorm room.

Needless to say, this was not one of my proudest moments. It definitely made me reconsider whom I was hanging out with, when, and where. Not to mention from that moment forward, if a guy claimed he had broken up with his girlfriend, I took the time to confirm **with her** that this was indeed the truth!

So how do you know if the man you're with is a *DOG FISH?* Read the *DOG FISH* characteristics below and place a check next to any sentence that pertains to your significant other.

DOG FISH Characteristics:

☐ Stares at your breasts instead of looking you in the eyes.

☐ Walks around a bar or club double-fisting drinks with his chest sticking out.

☐ Says things like, "By the end of the night that girl will be all over *this!*"

☐ Thinks ignoring or insulting women is a dating strategy.

☐ Checks out other women when he's with you.

☐ Learns sexual techniques from porn, rather than communicating with you about wants, needs, and desires.

☐ Calls you the wrong name during sex.

☐ Keeps naked pics of his ex-girlfriend/s.

☐ Is in a relationship with you, but continues to talk about other women he's slept with or dated.

☐ Tries to talk you into a three-some.

☐ Has cheated in the past (remember that past behavior is the best predictor of future behavior).

☐ Frequents strip clubs or has the belief that getting a blow-job from a stripper at a bachelor party is no big deal (after all—it is just a party favor).

☐ Thinks that what you don't know won't hurt you.

☐ Tells you that if you love him you'll sleep with him.

☐ Tells you that he doesn't use condoms because "it just doesn't feel good," but then assures you that he's (somehow) disease free.

☐ He tells you he's just not ready for a commitment, but would like to hang out and be friends and of course, sleep with you.

☐ Sends so many unsolicited dick pics that more people recognize his dick than his face.

If you put a check next to <u>one or more</u> of the above characteristics, then you might be with *DOG FISH*! *Three or more checks means immediate action is required*!

So, you've realized you're with a *DOG FISH*. Now what do you do? I think you already know the answer to this. You got it. . .THROW HIM BACK!!! Your future depends on it! If you're in a relationship with a *DOG FISH,* gather up your girlfriends, your favorite ice cream, and a bottle of wine (or three) and cry as much as you need to after you throw him back. But don't waste one more minute with this pond scum!

OCTOPUS

Mr. Grabby Hands

THESE GUYS SEEM TO HAVE multiple "go-go-gadget arms" that always have the need to touch every girl in close vicinity to them. There are two variations of Octopi. One is sly with a subtle approach and the other is bold with lightning fast tentacles.

Picture this: you're with the girls for a night out, and suddenly a guy approaches your group. He seems very charismatic, friendly, strikes up a good conversation, and makes everyone laugh. While he's interacting with you he inches closer and closer inside your circle. His arm makes its way around one girl's shoulders. His other tentacle is on another girl's back. Then an arm makes its way around someone's waist. In fifteen minutes or less this *OCTOPUS* has somehow touched at least 75% of the girls in your group in some way. He's sly about a quick brush of someone's breast or tush; you know, so it seems like an accident. His goal is to win over most or all of the girls of the group so no one will call him out on his subtle advances.

The second type of **OCTOPUS** is just outright brash and inappropriate. He's the type that smacks your ass as you walk by, or grabs your boob and then smiles at you like it was a compliment instead of a tasteless, disrespectful gesture.

SPRING BREAK-TO-PUS

One year in college, a bunch of the girls and I decided to go party-it-up at the beach for spring break. One of the clubs we went to was so jam-packed with people, you could barely move. You were forced to brush up against everyone you attempted to walk by. It was unbelievable the amount of Octopi that thought they had the right to slap, smack, and grab all parts of your body as you walked by them. I was getting so pissed. I told my girlfriend behind me, "*if one more guy grabs me I swear to God I'm going to punch him in the balls,*" I barely got that statement out of my mouth when a guy I was walking by grabbed my left breast and smacked my right ass cheek. My reaction was faster than the speed of light as I turned and gave an uppercut to his manhood. I only realized what I had actually done after the dude was lying on his back, holding his package and screaming. I stood over him and said, "*Maybe next time you'll think twice before you grab another girl like that.*"

PUBLIC TRANS-pOcTO-PUS

Allison was living in a major metropolitan city for a brief stint. On this particular day the subway was chock-full of people. Every stop was filled to the gills and people were packed in more tightly than a can of sardines; it was almost difficult to breathe! The carriage doors opened and Allison filed in just like everyone else. She got a foothold and grabbed a handrail. She had a long ride in this stuffy car and couldn't wait to get home. More people piled in at the next stop and at that moment, a guy from the last stop pressed up against her. She could feel his entire body against hers. Creepy. But what was even creepier is the guy had an erection and began pressing and rubbing against her.

She gave him the stink eye, but it did not deter him.

"What do you think you're doing?"

He pretended not to hear her.

Allison turned around to face the man and said in a VERY LOUD VOICE...

"Dude, you had better STOP rubbing your HARD DICK against me or there's going to be a HUGE PROBLEM to deal with."

Hard cock exited at the next stop.

You've attracted the tentacles of an *OCTOPUS* if:

☐ He's touched 60% of your body within 5 minutes of meeting you.

☐ He's touched the butts, thighs, and breasts of all of your girlfriends.

☐ Every picture taken with him in it shows his arm or hands on a different girl.

☐ His arm is around you, but is sure to leave the other free to cop a feel on someone else.

☐ If you call him out on being "too friendly" with your girlfriends, you're immediately labeled as jealous, insecure and are overreacting.

☐ Solicits nude pics from you.

You realize you're entangled in the tentacles of an *OCTOPUS*. Detach the suction cups and doggie paddle towards someone who will be more respectful of your body, and your friends'.

GOLD FISH

Materialistic Idiot with Superficial Priorities

WE DON'T NEED MUCH description here. These are the guys who spend exorbitant amounts of time and energy to give the appearance of wealth and prosperity through flashy materialism.

Some of them wear their own weight in gold and jewels as if they couldn't pick and choose – so instead they just chose them all. Others choose to emulate Haute-Couture fashion.

This could be the guy that bought the fully loaded BMW, but still lives with his parents. It's also the guy who is always buying shots for everyone at the bar, "Just put it on my tab" is his motto. He also tends to have a new tattoo, the newest iPhone or the latest technology gadget. Meanwhile he can't pay off his school loans and is near eviction because he can't pay his rent. The **GOLD FISH** tries to hide his insecurities by stroking his ego with external, materialistic showboating. He's also the one who posts on social media every hour so others can boost his ego with their responses.

Some might really have a lot of money to flaunt. The point here is that they're focusing on the external, rather than the internal. This is a red flag regarding where their priorities are and where they are in life. Let's face it, he's a *THROW BACK* if he's spending more money on flash than on practicalities, and even more so if he's taking advantage of other people in his life in order to be able to be flashy.

TAD

Tad invited me to dinner for our first date. We went to a trendy Asian Fusion restaurant that opened near my neighborhood. The food was delish, but Tad was not.

Tad had arrived well before I got there—which was very considerate, but he did that so he could hide all of the gifts he bought me. With gifts hidden, we introduced ourselves, said our pleasantries and had a look at the menu, which was pointless because Tad took it upon himself to order for me AND to order one of just about everything on the menu. Once our order was placed he began placing gift after gift on to the table! Really, I was NOT IMPRESSED.

My initial reaction was to wonder what he had to hide. Was the content of his character so lackluster that he had to distract me with STUFF in order to deter me from having a good look at HIM? The short answer was YES.

On another occasion, Tad asked me for my measurements. Did your jaw drop? Mine did! He said he wanted to have clothes made for me because he has seen some cute outfits that he'd like to see me in and wanted to have them made for me. If that wasn't strange enough, he contacts me one day to tell me that he commissioned an artist to generate some artwork for my house and had ordered some shrubbery for my garden. What?! Now, I am a pretty woman, but I was no *Pretty Woman*, so why was he treating me like one?!?!

This was just the tip of the iceberg with Tad; he was a man who was economical with the truth. Yes, truth economy—when someone doesn't flat out lie, but leaves out relevant information on purpose. People are *economical* with the information they give you so they can pursue their (hidden) agenda in a way that seems like they had your approval/agreement since they were "honest" and "open" with the information they gave you. How can anyone really give a seal of approval when they were sent off with only *some* of the facts?

I think you can imagine what dealing with Tad was like. He liked to get his way, and was probably used to getting his way, since what seemed like generosity was actually a way to set you up to owe him, to have to oblige him, to give in to his requests and demands. Only, I didn't <u>ask</u> him for any of the "stuff" he was trying to throw at me and I didn't owe him anything…and I let him know it.

I told him I was an independent woman who could think for herself and certainly did not need him to *take it upon himself* to make decisions *for me*; I could buy my own clothes; I could order my own meals; And… well you get the picture.

Now, a guy with half a brain could process this information… but not Tad. His reaction was that my feisty and determined demeanor was a turn on… and that when I talked like that… I gave him a… *boner*. I thought I was going to lose my lunch!! I mean, WTF?! That was downright inappropriate…not to mention demeaning and DISRESPECTFUL.

Clearly, I'm not the only woman he has used his delusions to court in this way. Once, he complained about his ex-girlfriend Clarissa because he said she was too materialistic and only wanted him for his money. I wonder where she learned to expect STUFF to be thrown her way?!

And ladies, I only met up with this guy three times! Yeah, three times too many! That *THROW BACK* took up way too much of my time, but I was very happy when he was back in the water. I threw him back and never fished there again! Whew!

There are a few lessons that came from the Tad experience. This guy was a degree holding professional, but he was a man without scruples. He tried to mask that by trying to buy people, which didn't make him happy, but with such fundamental flaws in his character, how else would he attract a woman *without* doing the long, hard work that it would have taken to work on himself? It was *much* easier to throw money their way.

He also held women to a standard he couldn't even meet himself; he told me that women were supposed to be a size six or smaller and needed to keep themselves fit to be attractive. This guy was a chub-a-lub, who had no right to dish out what he couldn't take. His views were very disrespectful to women because in reality he wanted arm candy who would go with *his* flow and not challenge him. When he was challenged he viewed it as charming, not serious, that the *little woman* had an opinion! He would then try to regain control through domination and machismo. He put up a good front—he talked the talk, but upon scratching past the surface it was immediately clear that it was lip service because he certainly could not walk the walk of a gentleman.

Now, I'm not saying a man shouldn't be generous! Quite the contrary! Generosity that is kind, bighearted, and considerate…generosity that is sincere, genuine and in tune with you as a person is sweet! Accept it (because you deserve it!) and reciprocate it (because he deserves the appreciation and his good deeds should not go unnoticed!). Recognize it because then you're on your way to finding your **Big Tuna**! Don't let insecure men who mask their issues with bling distract you from meeting a true **catch**!

J.R. & Nathan

J.R. idolizes anyone with money, if they're making six figures everything they do is gold in J.R.'s opinion. J.R. equates money with power. He thinks it's the magic potion to living the high life, a life defined by parties, debauchery, indulgence, extravagance, luxury, power, authority, influence, and ease. As long as they're raking in the cash, and living large, they're a success.

J.R. thinks Nathan is the bee's knees because of the car he drives, because he spends evenings hanging out as his own establishment, or because he has multiple business endeavors live at one time. What J.R. fails to acknowledge is that just because Nathan has these things, doesn't mean he's a winner. Nathan parties, meets beautiful women, takes them home, lavishes them with dinners, free drinks, and other indulgences, but that is all he has to offer. Nathan is a loyal man, he'll stand behind his friends, and he's a shrewd businessman, who has accumulated legitimate wealth as a result. He's also an emotional train wreck, who lives a life with no intimacy; really, a rather sorry and pathetic existence devoid of meaning and purpose.

Defining success in terms of wealth, position, or money is problematic. It doesn't take into account the intangibles – character, integrity, moral fiber, behavior, emotional and psychological maturity, or spirituality. Success solely defined EXTERNALLY, misses the mark. However, when success is defined as the ability to meet one's goals AND the definition reflects the person's integrity, you've got a more complete definition of what real success is. There are many successful people out there who don't boast six figures or more, but enjoy a success that Nathan and J.R. might never know.

Think of it like this…

What makes a Rolex so fabulous and desirable? It's impeccable craftsmanship inside **and** out. A *GOLD FISH* is like a knock-off… shiny on the outside, but lack-luster on the inside. If you've reeled in a *GOLD FISH* or worse yet, if a *GOLD FISH* has reeled you in – you've got FOOL'S GOLD! It's time to CUT THE LINE and keep on fishin'!

ROSE

Rose dated a guy who could only get together on Thursdays. Even after months of dating he wouldn't invite her to his house or to meet his friends. Why?! It turns out that he and his buddies lived in a cramped apartment, where they SHARED the payments on their sports car and on the designer suits that they SHARED with one another.

Some guys don't even go through the trouble that Rose's date went through. Some of them just mooch off of their overly-enabling family. Some stack up some pretty heavy credit card debt. Others are return kings; they go shopping at high-end places, wear the outfits a few times and then return it to the stores. Sometimes, return kings forget how much cash they've got in their wallets and the lucky sales clerk makes out big time!

Again, don't let the bling distract you! Figure out what is behind the bling. Is it all ego? Are they diverting your attention to their STUFF because they don't want you to look at THEM?

A *GOLD FISH* will spend more time on appearances than on himself. Rather than work on being the better man from the inside out, he prefers to decorate the outside, hoping you won't ever want to have a look inside. A **CATCH** doesn't do this – a **CATCH** is in balance and is in a place to invite you into his life.

Finally, male *GOLD FISH* attract female gold diggers and then complain about them! They ridicule the women who will play the arm candy game with them and resent the very women that they attract. This is so laughable and is extremely hypocritical. It is the law of attraction in action – you don't attract what you want in life, you attract what you ARE. *GOLD FISH* deserve gold diggers – it's what they ask for!

He might be a *GOLD FISH* if:

☐ He spends more $ on the studs in his ears than on his rent.

☐ His mouth puts the 1848 Gold Rush to shame.

☐ You need to wear sunglasses to reduce the glare when looking at him.

☐ He doesn't own much (or any) of what he sports.

☐ He didn't remove the item's tag so he could take it back to the store.

☐ His self-worth is directly linked to what he owns/showboats.

☐ Values money more than integrity.

☐ Thinks a flashy car buys him character.

☐ Thinks Cristal buys class.

☐ Sends unsolicited dick pics of random dicks that he tries to pass off as his own.

JELLYFISH

THE SPINELESS MOMMA'S BOY

H ERE'S THE TWIST TO THIS FISH. . .when Mommy is around he is very attentive, communicative and fun-loving; in a 12-year old boy kind of way. He listens to her, but not to you. He comes when Mommy calls, but ignores you. He answers her calls on the first ring and talks for extended periods of time. He may or may not call you or answer when you call him. He does things like: goes to her house to pull weeds, put up her Christmas tree, run errands for her, put away heavy platters. . .that yes, her own husband is very capable of doing.

You might have thought he was a good **catch** at first, when you saw he was sweet and respectful to his mother. However, as time goes on you begin to see that his mother controls him, like crack controls a drug-addict.

Unless you're okay with always being second best and settling for a coward, who will never set healthy boundaries and limitations for

Mommy-dearest, then you better run for cover and hit the deck. The mother of a mama's boy has the potential to be very dangerous, explosive and extremely controlling, although this isn't necessarily obvious at first. This relationship you'll find, is not a relationship at all. How can it be when much of his time is spent doting over a woman who still treats him like he's a little boy? If he doesn't have emotional maturity and is treated like a little kid, then he is definitely a *THROW BACK*. Who wants to compete with somebody's mother for God sake?! The worst part is that his behaviors will slowly change yours into becoming mommy-number-two for him. Eeewwww!!!

Remember, you are NEVER supposed to fight over the **catch**. This includes fighting over the **catch** with someone's mother. No man is ever worth that. THIS RELATIONSHIP WILL LEAVE YOU FEELING LIKE NOTHING LESS THAN A FISH OUT OF WATER.

Have you ever been with a guy where you ask him a question and he literally just ignores you and doesn't answer? Or gets up from the dinner table after eating the meal you cooked for him, says nothing, and leaves his plate and all of the mess for you to clean up while he goes to the couch to watch TV or play video games?

Did you partner with a man that doesn't attend any of your family events, even though you go to all of his?

This type of fish is too cowardly to communicate with you when something is wrong, but then blames you for not knowing what ails him.

This fish might pay a decent amount of attention to you at first, but seems submerged in silence once he feels as though he's reeled you in. Now, he may continue to give you his affections periodically, but if you pay close attention, you'll notice it's only when he'll benefit from it. So basically, when he wants something, he's into you and seems like the most affectionate guy in the world. When he doesn't need you or want something from you, he's cold, aloof, non-communicative, affectionless and distant. BUT… he's never that way with mommy!

JACK

Jack seemed like a very chill, laid back considerate kind of guy. He did a lot of nice things for me during the courting phase of our relationship. He actually made statements like, "I would never live too, too close to my parents. I moved an hour away so we could still have a good relationship, but not have to see each other constantly. A healthy distance is always good." Well as our relationship became serious over time, he wanted to buy a house and move ten minutes away from his mother. Unfortunately, I didn't know at the time to listen to my intuition. It screamed "no," but I, like many young women, thought I was being inflexible and unreasonable if I refused. I can tell you that once we lived near his mother, our relationship went to hell. That woman pretended to be pleasant, friendly and generous. But she made moves to exert her control over how she thought we should live our lives. She stopped by unannounced and uninvited because "something was bothering her." She would then sit us down, like little children and lecture us and scold us. What would Jack do? NOTHING. He set no boundaries and no limits on this crazy woman. When she said, "jump" he jumped. Then she would criticize him and say it wasn't high enough, and he'd jump again. We could have planned an entire day together, but if his mother called, it all flew out the window so he could tend to her controlling needs. He could be very affectionate and tender one minute, but if his mother was around he kept his distance from me.

The most important thing I learned from the relationship was to listen to my intuition when it's telling me something. If I had listened to my internal guidance system, then I wouldn't have had to endure being overlooked by my significant other or have his mother constantly competing with me for Jack's time, attention, and affections.

CARSON & CARRIE

Carson had a nine-to-five that made him a decent living. He had a modest sized home he invested some sweat-equity into. He had a nice sized yard that invited summer time picnics and barbeques. When Carrie met him, summer was winding down and she was invited to join him and his friends for the final back yard grilling and barbeques of the season.

Everything seemed normal at first. The gatherings around the fire pit were pleasant. Carson's friends seemed to be decent people and his family seemed to be close knit, but something was... *off*.

Almost every time Carrie and Carson were in contact, Carson was with his mother. There was always some "reason" for it. His mother didn't drive so Carson was the go-to guy and was in charge of taking her to run errands. She always needed help with one thing or another. She couldn't even get something out of storage on her own. Carson literally chose to map his life around his mother.

When Carrie would call about a get-together, Carson would want to play it by ear because his mother might need him, or they would have to make plans for after he saw his mother.

At this point Carrie was still trying not to judge him. Tired by the many *THROW BACKS* she had encountered, she didn't want to rush to judgment, but still knew she had to pay attention to those little warning signs. Well, judgment day came and it came fast and hard!

Carrie was invited to have dinner with the family. After about a month of get-togethers and BBQs, it was time for mommy's approval.

The spread was plentiful. There was food for a feast and for everyone's appetite. All of it was home cooked by his mother. The table was set and when they were called to be seated, Carson's mom not only made him his plate, but she also took it upon herself to CUT HIS FOOD FOR HIM.

OMG... is she going to CHEW it for him too? Or put his napkin on his lap for him? Or lick her finger to clean off his face? What's next in the twilight zone?

You're probably wondering... but she did not chew his food or clean his face for him... but she DID do his laundry that night and she did cater to his every whim... fussing over keeping his lemonade topped off... fussing over keeping his plate full and getting him his favorite desserts.

When mommy called Carson, he snapped to it like a good little (thirty year old) boy. When any other woman entered that scenario there was no room for them in Carson's life. While Carson was unable to cut the cord, Carrie, my friends, was NOT!

Oh Nelly, you're with a *JELLY* if:

☐ He's not comfortable showing affection.

☐ His mom still cuts his meat.

☐ Mommy still does his laundry.

☐ After he finishes in the bathroom he yells, "Mom! I'm done" so she can come wipe his ass.

☐ Mom shows up at your house (unannounced) around twice a week.

☐ He lets his mom borrow his car to take long trips, but throws a fit when you need it because yours is in the shop.

☐ He'll answer his mother's phone call even in the middle of sex.

☐ Before you leave for a family event he asks you, "Is that what you're wearing?" But the first words he mutters to his mother are, "you look so beautiful," even when she looks awful.

☐ He doesn't communicate well, but expects you to still know what's on his mind.

☐ He's hot one minute, cold the next.

☐ He seems to get along with everyone, but when you dig a little deeper, you realize it's a façade due to his fear of being rejected or disliked by others.

☐ He shows very little appreciation for who you are or what you do for him.

☐ He's not someone who will make you feel protected or who will stand up for you.

If you now realize you've got a *JELLY* lurking beneath the waves, tread towards a rescue boat powered by your closest friends or family before you get stung and sink into the dark depths of the sea!

PILOT FISH

THE SIDE-KICK

Picture this: ladies night out. You see a guy approaching from across the room coming over to test the waters. This is the *PILOT FISH*. He's scouting out you and your friends in order to report back to the guys about whether or not they'll stand a chance with you. It doesn't matter if he strikes out because his real purpose is to test the waters for his buddies. On the one hand, in order to compete among the more voracious fish, he needs to get in there first so he doesn't get overlooked by the ladies once his buddies come swimming around. On the other hand, the more voracious fish want him to go first because he makes them look more impressive after the ladies have met the low man on the totem pole.

Sometimes a *PILOT FISH* is just along for the ride. If bunches of BLOWFISH are vying for a certain *THROW BACK*, the *PILOT FISH* is bound to score with one of them. So, he'll let his buddies' pair up and THEN figure out who he can hook. His making it seem like he *wasn't* looking, makes him look like a "good guy," but this is part of his game, so be aware of his tactics.

Doug

I went out with a couple of girls from work to celebrate Pamela's birthday. While ordering drinks, we saw a group of about twelve guys enter the club. After about seven minutes of checking us out from a distance I saw their designated *PILOT FISH* break away from the group. As he made his way toward us, I turned to Pam and asked, "Why do they have to send the *PILOT FISH* first?!"

PILOT FISH, immediately introduced himself to the ladies the guys were trying to bait and wasted no time boasting about his career accomplishments. As he failed to impress them, the other fish began to dog paddle their way over, to try to get their turn. As they carefully worked their way into the conversation and became more involved and interested in the ladies, the *PILOT FISH,* slowly drifted out to sea. Doug tried with all his might, but he was swimming against the current and with his eyes on the prize he tried desperately to reel in the catch. His efforts were in vain because the catch had set her sights on another fish.

The Three Stooges

Another role of Pilot Fish is to keep fish they are currently hitting on in play, while the more dominant members of the school try their chances with other fish who are fresh on the scene.

One night we were out at a nightclub that was packed to the gills. We finally spotted two open seats around a fire pit. Trying not to impede upon the group already socializing there, we scooted to the far end of the pit and talked amongst ourselves. Rather immediately three guys tried to make eye contact and began to avert their attention away from the two ladies they had been sitting with. Shortly after whispers, elbow nudges and text messages, the *PILOT FISH* flew into action. As Dominant Fish #1 got up to go to the bar, the *PILOT FISH* took his seat to distract the two girls and keep them in play. In the meantime, Dominant Fish #2 moved towards us, leaving room for Dominant Fish #1's return. Fish #1 returned with an eyebrow-raise and a smile. Although, impressed with how skillfully they maneuvered these tactics, it was time to remove ourselves from the situation; we were both in relationships at the time and we don't fight over a "catch" anyway... if they were doing this to them they'd definitely do it to us at some point.

Hopefully, those two girls were insightful enough to see what was really going on and made the choice to throw them back! I mean, how insulting for those guys to be rude enough to strategically ditch them as soon as they saw someone else.

He's a *PILOT FISH* if:

☐ He's the runt of the group.

☐ He's first to approach and first to (unwillingly) leave.

☐ He carries out the orders of the Big Fish.

☐ He's not part of the decision-making process.

SHARK

THE EMOTIONALLY UNAVAILABLE PREDATOR

THIS IS THE GUY WHO ALWAYS looks the part by dressing well, drives a nice car, and has a decent or even exceptional bankroll. His smile is stunning and comes across as generous early on in a relationship.

The *SHARK* demonstrates dangerous secrecy; he is a calculating predator who uses his charm to suck girls in. Ladies, men who have nothing to hide, *HIDE NOTHING*. If he goes out of his way to keep many things in his life a secret, this is a huge red flag. I don't care how wonderful he seemed or how much you initially bragged to your friends about how generous he has been to you. If you start to see signs your man is hiding things from you, he is most likely a *SHARK*. The things he might be hiding could be dangerous to you physically, emotionally, and mentally. If he's hiding promiscuity, for example, this could bring sexually transmitted diseases your way. Lack of true communication can cause emotional stress and mental anguish; mistrust that develops from secrecy.

There is one question to ask ladies— why the heck bother? So, this (seemingly) successful, captivating, charismatic guy that you thought was wonderful at first, turned out to be a conniving, emotionally unavailable, bastard. There are plenty of fish in the sea, right? SO THROW HIM BACK AND KEEP FISHING!! Life is way too short to keep one rotting fish around to stink up your life! You'll get over it! The longer you stay with a *SHARK,* the harder it is to recover from it. He's manipulative and will turn his misdoings around onto you, to make it seem like you're the bad person or the one in the wrong. He can even sometimes convince you that YOU are the one who has a problem because you are "checking up on him" or angry at him when he just wants to "enjoy the day." He might try to convince you your "crazy trust issues" are ruining the relationship when the actual problem is that he hides emails, phone calls, texts, or posts, and/or is inconsistent in accounting for his whereabouts. *SHARKs* harbor discontent about being in relationships, BUT relationships are the perfect place for them to feed their control addiction AND can be used to help them climb the ladder. If you express unhappiness with him on any level, he ruthlessly attacks with something that might have bothered him months prior, just so he can turn the negative attention onto you instead of onto him.

The *SHARK*'s covertness should NOT be ignored! Ladies, you need to tune into your instincts on this one! There will be brief feelings of doubt, confusion, or a subtle, "this just doesn't feel right for some reason." Don't ignore these!! When with a *SHARK* the most powerful defense a woman has is her own intuition. Unfortunately, this tends to be ignored until it's too late. You don't need to justify or explain yourself away to everyone else when you pay attention to those red flags. Just throw him back and move on. The longer you waste your time on a *SHARK* the less time you have to find your **Big Tuna**.

That's right! *SHARKS* always have their game faces on because they always have a plan. As mentioned, these guys are either at or want to be at the top of the food chain, are successful, (or striving to be) and they'll let you know it! Don't let the suit and tie fool you—it's part of how they gain power and maintain status. Don't let the flashy title fool you! They're cunning and manipulative. They'll make demands and expect you to indulge in them. But watch out!! No matter how many hoops you jump through, it will never be enough to win his heart. *SHARK*s tend to be emotionally unavailable because, again, their personal life and their business lives are one and the same. In fact, if you protest he'll respond by ignoring you or insulting you (after all—resistance is not part of the plan). Look out because *SHARK*s will work long hours to score whatever it is they've got in their sights. Superficially, this makes them look hard working and diligent, but take a deeper look so you won't be fooled.

Rule of thumb — if you spot a fin GET THE HELL OUT OF THE WATER!

RYAN & EMILY

Meet Ryan, the emotionally unavailable great white. Don't get me wrong, Ryan is an emotional guy, he just has no interest in YOUR emotions. Ryan is a *SHARK* trying hard to swim amongst other *SHARK*s and anyone or anything that gets in the way of that is chum. How does he manage to keep his focus? He tries to control everything and I mean everything.

Ryan controlled the flow of information. He was very selective about the information he shared about his businesses and how he would discuss them. He was always economical with the truth, either through aggrandizement and exaggeration, or by down-playing the things he didn't want people to know. Ryan and Emily had started a business together, a business that never would have been launched had it not been for her credit. Ryan was mountain high in school debt and couldn't get the business or personal loans to foot the cost so Emily took on the risk for the both of them. Being the *SHARK* he was, when one of their first deals was about to close, Ryan announced to everyone,

"My partners just told me my deal is officially closing in a few weeks!!"

To which everyone began to congratulate **him** and tell him how great **he** was! Emily chimed in to let everyone know that it wasn't "his" deal, that "he" didn't act alone, rather it was THEIR deal because they BOTH had ownership in the business, therefore the deal pertained to the TWO OF THEM.

Ryan, knowing full well they worked as a team, and that none of it would have been possible had it not been for Emily and the fact that she was the one that assumed the risk, replied with,

"Thanks for the help, love, and support. I couldn't have done it without you."

Her help, love, and support?! What?! How about *thank you for your 50% of the work so this deal got done?!* You see? The *SHARK* exaggerates his role, down plays everyone else's, to try to boost his status. There's no gratitude in that pompous response and there's no recognition. Rather, he attempted to take all the praise for himself, but was foiled when Emily chimed in.

Part of the reason they have to control everything is because they have insecurities - so they often feel inferior to others.

Ryan even tried to control their sex life. Ryan would engage in what's called solo sex. That is, he'd jerk off regularly to satisfy his own needs and to avoid intimacy, but would come to Emily for comfort contact, that is, for cuddling and close contact. When Emily would become irritable after weeks or more of only cuddling, and annoyed by the fact he was more than willing to take care of his needs on a regular basis, but not hers, Ryan would have a fit. "What am I supposed to do? WAIT until you're done with work?" *Um, yeah. It's called impulse control. It's called wanting to connect with your partner. It's called WANTING to take care of someone else's needs! It's called – getting joy from being together! It's called INTIMACY!*

He blamed Emily for this. He told her she was too interested in sex and came onto him too much, which just put pressure on him to perform.

Then, when she'd wait for him to approach her, he whined that it put too much pressure on him to always initiate it. What does this sound like - hoop jumping! *If only Emily would get it right they'd have a sex life… but she keeps getting it wrong so it is HER fault that there's trouble in the bedroom (not the fault of the emotionally unavailable, intimacy fearing SHARK)!*

When Emily confronted him about the problems, the hoop jumping, etc. Ryan, handled it like a true **SHARK** and told Emily that it boiled down to this:

"You know I'm going to do what I want, when I want, and with whoever I want and you can't stop me. I won't be controlled."

Ryan exercised this philosophy regularly and he launched that business because his dream career wasn't going as he thought it should go. He needed to be involved in something more reliable and stable that would enable him to stand on his own two feet, and still be in a position to build toward his dream job. When it came to his dream job, Ryan could NOT be relied on to make rational decisions. He was way too emotionally driven by the topic. Those desires drove every decision he would make, but his declarations were unusual, given that he had no formal experience beyond course work and workshops.

When he started taking a class he couldn't afford, it's no surprise how often his attachment to that class got in the way of a healthy relationship with Emily, and how often his, *do what he wants attitude,* came into play.

"I need a place to work and you can't be here."

"Ok, why can't I be here? We have more than one room, I can go in the other room if you need to hold a meeting."

"Because I need to be able to be free and focused and if I'm worrying about you in that process it's going to fuck it up."

Ok – now people, who have nothing to hide, hide nothing. So, this is a huge RED FLAG.

"I'm sorry, but what could you POSSIBLY be doing at a business meeting that you wouldn't be divulging to your other colleagues? That IS what this is about and are you REALLY telling me you might be doing something or saying something that you wouldn't say in front of me, and would be doing so with a female colleague in our apartment?"

Ryan had a screaming fit about how Emily wasn't supportive and was getting in the way of his career. So, Emily knowing that people who have nothing to hide, HIDE NOTHING, allowed Ryan to have his "private" meetings. As soon as they were scheduled, she left the house, but she left a recording device on while she was gone and listened to every word they said!

What was Ryan hiding? Apparently a lot...

How about the fact they kissed? What did the partner, who had a boyfriend at the time, say about it? *How important it was for them to communicate with their bodies.* No wonder he insisted on private meetings! He was setting the stage for cheating, under the excuse of career building. Only, he knew he couldn't get away with that if Emily were home! He had to find a way to get her out. Ryan denies this happened to this very day – true to his *SHARK* nature, he tries to manipulate everyone into believing Emily is unreasonable and controlling, and unsupportive of his career. The only thing is – he doesn't know that he was caught on tape discussing the very thing that "never happened."

How about the fact he took his shirt off during a meeting? With Emily there he could NEVER take off that shirt and show off the work he'd been doing with the workout videos he bought himself for Emily's birthday!

How about the conversation they had about drinking water tasting like cum? She was the one who took him to buy that water in the first place. They met up without Emily knowing about it, so she could introduce him to this fabulous water, only a short time later to declare it tasted funny?!

"It tastes funny... it tastes, like, you know... like a man..."

"No, I don't know... what does that taste like."

"It tastes like after you've had him in your mouth."

"Oh, well some men just drink pineapple juice for that."

"I so LOVE where this conversation is going, Ryan."

Oh, yes, totally appropriate (you caught the sarcasm, right?), Ryan. The kicker in this is that Ryan once had a screaming fit at Emily for having a "flirtatious and inappropriate" conversation with a wealthy businessman they knew.

"I can't believe the two of you FLIRTING like that."

"Um, Ryan, what the FUCK are you talking about? I was telling him about my WORK PROJECT."

"You were FLIRTING. Shamelessly flirting and it's bullshit."

Yeah, ok, Ryan. Emily can't have a professional discussion about her **professional interests** *in public,* but Ryan can talk about blow jobs behind closed doors and in a context where Emily was not allowed to be around?!

Did you all say what I think you said? YEP!! *THROW BACK!!*

What are the lessons? People, who have nothing to hide, hide nothing. *SHARK*S are emotionally unavailable, and this distresses your friendship, your relationship, and your sex life. *SHARK*S seek power so they try to control everything and will only associate with people they think they can control. Whenever they sense they cannot fool someone, they'll retreat in search of easier prey. They'll move from one thing to the next in an attempt to reach the top of the food chain, or to at least keep up such appearances. In fact, Ryan used to read about body language and lying. He was actively researching the cues that indicate lying so he would be more believable when he was telling his lies!

*SHARK*S are all TEETH. They're bite is deadly, so stay out of their way because their emotionally juvenile, ego-driven, control-freak, TOXIC mantra is always at play…

SHARKS do what they want, when they want, and with whom they want… they cannot be guided to healthier shores.

Don't waste your time! CUT THE LINE and listen to your instincts. *SHARKS* are manipulative and do a great job making it look like YOU'RE the problem. Essentially, they're gaslighting. Upon closer inspection, however, many times they're just trying their damnedest to keep the upper hand. If you're told you're over reacting, or your gut tells you something more is going on, LISTEN TO IT. *SHARKS* are masters at getting what they want. When your internal bells go off, LISTEN to them chime. Take note and then take action.

SHARKS:

- ☐ Well dressed.
- ☐ Business – executive types (or wanna-bes).
- ☐ Controlling, secretive, and cold in relationships.
- ☐ Demanding, selfish, huge ego.
- ☐ Power hungry (in every sense of the term).
- ☐ Emotionally unavailable.
- ☐ Can't be reasoned with.
- ☐ Unilateral Decision-Maker: He leaves you out of the decision-making in favor of dictating how things will be done.
- ☐ Does what he wants, when he wants, how he wants, and with whom he wants.
- ☐ Prefers to send a video of him jerking off because dick pics are a downgrade.

THE BAR JACK

THE HEAVY DRINKER

Yes, this is a real fish, and they do come in the human variety. You know because you've probably spotted them, the aging male who hangs out at the bar on a regular basis, oftentimes from happy hour until closing. He visits all the local watering holes and greets all of his (drinking) buddies. **BAR JACK**s have a lot of female "friends" and are inclined to date women who are <u>much</u> younger than they are because they think settling down is too restricting since love should be free and he should be free to love all. This is partially due to the fact that they can't seem to remember who or when they've made a commitment to someone. Many **BAR JACK**s try to have committed relationships, but they fail because commitment and all that it entails for a solid, healthy partnership, interferes with their partying. In all actuality the **BAR JACK** is committed to, you guessed it, the bar scene.

It is important to recognize the underlying philosophy of the *BAR JACK*. *BAR JACK*s do not seek the affection or the attention of women their own age. This is because women in the same age bracket have learned enough life lessons to be intolerant of various forms of bad behavior. While a girl in her early twenties is most likely flattered, the 30 something year-olds tend to be more cautious, the 40 somethings are precocious and have the wisdom to refuse the advances of the *BAR JACK*. Now do you understand why *BAR JACK*s would chase younger women? Their naivety due to lack of life experience makes them easier to prey upon.

EMMA & EDWARD

Emma fell head over heels for a Bar Jack. Only, at the time no one knew he was a Bar Jack. Emma and Edward are close in age so when they met the fact they were enjoying the bar scene and the occasional pub-crawl was pretty normal. Emma was a beauty, tall, thin, dark hair and dark eyes. She's the kind of woman who makes friends easily and is liked by everyone. Edward is very likeable as well. He's social, loves to be around people, and loves to talk about a variety of subjects. The two were a great pair! They enjoyed some of the same activities, their friends liked one another, and their respective social networks easily meshed. The problem, though, was that Edward was a Bar Jack. When their friendship began to turn into a relationship, Edward would pull away. When things would get back on the upswing, Edward would shake things up again. As Emma was naturally moving into the next phase of a relationship, the Bar Jack she reeled in was fighting to get back to the water. The Bar Jack's primary relationship is with the bar scene, and anyone or anything that keeps him from that will be cast-off. The Bar Jack swims in that pond and that pond alone and will only seek out other fish that will swim there with him. The women Edward dated were always younger, that way he could continue to be on the scene, and he had a "legitimate" excuse to be well into his forties and still in bars on evenings and weekends. Emma got wise to this situation and she cut the line. She was and is a catch! Some lucky man is going to find his **Angel Fish** in her!

Watch out for *Bar Jacks*! While some could be full-fledged alcoholics, some might be functional alcoholics. A functional alcoholic is one who doesn't seem to have a problem. By all appearances they seem to have their lives under control. They have a hard time believing they might have a problem because they're (relatively) successful and just drink to unwind, relax, or socialize. However, if they're never without a drink, they just might have a problem.

BAR JACK Characteristics:

☐ Is only happy at happy-hour.

☐ Always has a drink in hand.

☐ If he doesn't already own a bar, then it's probably his lifelong dream to own one.

☐ Always has an open tab and encourages you to have "just one more."

☐ The older he gets, the younger the women he solicits.

☐ Doesn't know what precocious means, but knows he doesn't want it in a woman.

☐ Accepts fake I.D.'s at face value.

☐ Might send a dick pick if whiskey dick doesn't rear its ugly head.

PUFFER FISH

THE POT HEAD

Potheads conjure up a number of images – from dropouts, to hippies, to gamers, to corporates, to jocks, to metal heads, and nerds! A lot of people like the wacky weed and there have been a lot of movements out there for the legalization of the drug, which in some states have been actualized. You'll not be hard-pressed to find a social group with herb at its center. There's a myth that marijuana isn't harmful, and perhaps that idea sparks from the fact that this plant has medicinal qualities. It does have some wonderful medicinal qualities if farmed and utilized in responsible ways. Although marijuana can have its place for people with serious medical conditions most recreational users drift into an addiction without even realizing it. It comes down to the role the drug plays in a person's life. Many will think they're not addicted since they don't smoke every day. That is the seductive danger with mota; it'll trick you into believing you don't have a problem, but as soon as you try to break it off, you end up realizing it has a hold on you. Furthermore, watch out for those peole who 'use' on a regular or fairly regular basis and ask – Are they doing so to suppress feelings and past emotional pains they never dealt with? Numbing your feelings is a dysfunctional coping mechanism that leads to superficial relationships that lack depth.

ROY & RAVEN

Roy insisted he didn't have a problem but Raven knew when he had been hiding his smoking because he developed a cough OR he'd jump out of bed in the middle of the night screaming at the ghosts that were messing with him. *Funny how those ghosts never bothered him on the days he hadn't toked up.*

One night, Roy woke up screaming at the top of his lungs. "Get out! Get out of here! Leave me alone." He shoved Raven out of bed and onto the floor, before jumping to his feet to confront the ghost in the room that had been tapping his legs. "You're not welcome here. Leave me alone. Get out." He told Raven how they wouldn't leave him alone again, convinced the ghosts were real, and were really there. It never occurred to him that these visits only happened after he came off of a high, and that he was actually experiencing hallucinations from the weed. He would tell people how ghosts haunted him and they followed him everywhere, but Raven knew the truth. She was living with him – wasn't a smoker, and was able to view the situation with a clear mind.

Roy said he was a recreational user and controlled his use; it didn't control him. He smoked because he wanted to, not because he had to. *The man used to get high in his car and would hide his smoking from Raven.* Yet, he never managed to quit for more than a few days at a time. It was inevitable that if he was stressed, frustrated, worried, or his head was racing with thoughts, the rolling papers were around. Any time he tried to quit, he would just get irritable, have trouble sleeping, or would feel depressed and would end up giving in. *Classic signs of withdrawal.* Talking to him about it was out of the question, and when she asked him how often he got high, he'd tell her he just did it once and a while for a good time. *This was a total lie.*

The truth was he was high more days out the week than he was not. This was not an observation Roy could accept and when Raven would try to address it he would blow her off, saying she was judgmental, controlling, and just wouldn't let him be who he was (another typical stance that addicts take). Roy would rant that Raven was keeping him from an active social life, when she wasn't keen on hanging out with stoner friends or when she asked him if it were a good idea for someone in Marijuana Anonymous to go hang out with heavy pot smokers. *Hanging out with other addicts normalizes the behavior and only makes it harder to quit because he's around others who readily justify the practice. It makes it that much easier for Roy to deny he has a problem on his hands.*

Clearly, he **wasn't** a recreational user and clearly he **couldn't** take it or leave it. He used it as an escape, as a way to deal with difficult situations or feelings. He used it to "clear his head," to relax, and to disengage. How he described his use to others was mismatched when it came to his actual practice. Like many others who struggle in this way, his perceptions didn't match reality. *These are clear signs of a person with a problem.*

Unfortunately, it is unpopular to discuss the dark side of marijuana, but it is a drug like any other and its misuse and abuse is real. Many people who are addicted don't even realize they have a problem because of the soft nature of the plant. Here's the lesson:

We're not here to take a 'yay' or 'nay' black and white approach to marijuana use. The choice to use is yours and so are the consequences (both good and bad). We're not denying the beauty of the plant and all that is has to offer. What we are telling you is that too much of anything can be unhealthy. Unfortunately with marijuana, it is much easier to become addicted than people currently want to acknowledge. The immediate effects are it impacts the brain directly; it distorts clear thinking, and alters perceptions. It also allows you to disengage so you cannot be intimately, emotionally present with your partner or loved ones.

Long-term use can result in attention and memory issues AND has measurable and predictable effects that interfere with the user's ability to pursue goals. Research shows that regular users have lower mental and physical health than their non-using counterparts, they have less academic and career success as compared to non-users, they have problems in relationships, have more job turn over, and those who started using in adolescence showed deficits in learning and had lower IQs. Chronic use is believed to be tied to mental illness and mental health disorders later on in life.

Roy has chosen not to break up with *MaryJane*. He heads to the cannabis club and buys himself some treats, but once the affair is over, he feels frustrated and ashamed she has such a strong hold on him. He tries to compensate by playing brain games to help keep his memory from deteriorating any further, and engages in other exercises to try to build brain power, but still refuses to address the reason behind the urgency to work on those cognitive activities. The last he spoke about it with Raven, she was strictly prohibited from voicing concern or trying to keep him on track. He rejects concern because he refuses to be accountable. He knows there is a bigger problem that he is afraid to confront directly, even with Raven's support. So, Raven swam to clear waters, while Roy swam to the warm waters of the bong bowl.

The *PUFFER FISH*:

☐ Thinks what he says makes sense after smoking pot.

☐ Says he's a recreational user who can take it or leave it, every few days.

☐ Believes he's not addicted because he didn't smoke yesterday.

☐ Thinks it's a cool part of his lifestyle, but still goes to MA.

☐ Surrounds himself with tokers so he can feel justified.

☐ Is disrespectful or verbally abusive to you because you DON'T smoke. He may call you a prude, goody-two-shoes, stuck-up or claim you think you're better than others.

☐ Tells you you're judgmental when you're only concerned with the possible negative side effects of his heavy use of weed.

☐ Laughs uncontrollably at nothing, literally nothing, but when you take him to a comedy show sober, he says it was boring.

☐ He's asked you four times what someone's name is and still can't remember. He then writes the name on his hand, only to look at it later and ask you, "How did this get here? And who is this anyway?!"

☐ He is emotionally unavailable and doesn't have the skills to gain emotional intimacy with you.

THE LEECH

HE'LL SUCK THE ENERGY & THE LIFE RIGHT OUT OF YOU!

THE *LEECH*'S GOAL IS to weasel his way into your life, often while eating you out of house and home, running up your bills, and using your appliances. He also often asks you if he can do his laundry at your place, over-stays his welcome, and simply seems to never want to leave.

Important to note: this is also the guy who subtly marks his "territory" to fend off any potential **Big Tunas** from coming around! Be careful because the *LEECH* can suck the life right out of you!

The *LEECH* reminds me of three different men. Before I describe them, I have to explain a few things. During the time of these three stories, I lived by myself (with my two dogs) in a large, beautiful four-bedroom house, in a lovely residential neighborhood. Since I had recently moved to the area I didn't have friends or family close by; they were all scattered across the state. With two dogs to take care of, it wasn't easy for me to make visits, so I often offered up my spare bedrooms to visitors instead. Whoever stayed over had the privacy of a single room and a full bathroom. It seemed like the perfect setup so they didn't have the burden of driving hours to come and see me, and then have to turn around and drive a distance to go back home. For example, it was great for my friend Cal, since coming to hang out with me meant he had to take a bus from Philly. Understanding this leads to my story about the first *LEECH* I sometimes still have nightmares about...

Nat

Nat is a guy I had known since high school. We had been pretty close back in the day and kept in touch with each other off and on since. He had accepted a job about an hour away from my house and we reconnected. I was ecstatic.

At first it seemed great to spend a lot of time with someone I had known for so long. We laughed and had fun together and saw each other often. Since he had to drive such a distance to come hang out with me, I offered him the same thing I offered all of my other friends, the option of staying over with use of the spare bedroom and bath. Nat jumped at the chance and ended up staying over almost every time he came to my house. Again, this was fun at first, but slowly and surely, he showed signs of being a *LEECH*.

It started when he asked if he could keep some of his clothes and personal items in my spare bedroom since he stayed over fairly often. I didn't think it was a big deal at the time so I said "*sure.*" That 'yes' led to constant calls, a bombardment of text messages and the request that I text him everyday before work, during my lunch break, after work, and then before going to bed. Ummm, what?!

He also began attempting to invite himself along when I had plans with other friends. Now, this was after we had already spent a couple of days a week together or had already planned activities two weekends in a row! He actually got frustrated when I told him that I couldn't hang out because I had other plans. Frusrated?! He had just spent two weekends in a row at my place! He would say stuff like, "*yeah, that sounds like fun. I wouldn't mind meeting them and hanging out with them. Maybe we could all do something together.*" Then he would magically somehow be in the area hanging out with other friends when that weekend came around and would call and try to persuade me to have us all meet up somewhere.

Typically, I wouldn't bother answering my phone because I was getting sick of him requiring so much attention and showing signs of being a possessive person. Remember, he was not even my boyfriend and he was behaving in this manner!!

When I would address the matter afterwards, he would tell me I was a bad friend because I wouldn't hang out with him when he was in the area. Once he even claimed I had put him at risk for getting into an accident because his designated driver got drunk and couldn't drive them home safely. He claimed he was calling so he could have a place to crash that night instead of having to go all the way to Philly with a drunken person driving. Funny he didn't reveal any of that in the moment . . . and this was *my* problem why?! His choice to ride with a drunk driver was *my* fault *how?*

Further, he would bring magazines to my house, that obviously had his name and mailing address on them, and leave them on my coffee and kitchen tables. This didn't seem like such a big deal at first, but then I realized this was an attempt to mark what he was trying to claim as his territory. He wanted any other fish that swam into my fish bowl, to see that he, Nat, was spending time with me.

He also would ask things like, "*Man, do I need to see a chiropractor. My back is killing me. Who do you go to? Hey do you know of a good dentist I could go to? Who's your dentist? Where do you work out? What's the name of your gym again?*" Next thing I knew he was going to my chiropractor, had taken a tour of my gym, had inquired about membership fees, and was looking into finding a dentist in my area.

This *LEECH* was a man who made a higher income than I did. He lived in an apartment that was barely half of what my mortgage was. He drove a company car and didn't pay for gas, tolls, or meals because they were considered company expenses! Yet, he would shower at my house, use all of my products, eat my food, ask for my toothpaste (I guess because he was too cheap or lazy to bring his own when he stayed over!), occasionally do his laundry (of course using my detergents, fabric softeners and dryer sheets), ask to borrow my E-Z Pass to pay for tolls his company already paid for, and then would try to weasel his way into my "community activities," like the chiropractor and the gym (among other things!).

One day I overheard part of a conversation he was having on the phone. I heard him saying something about his plans "*to move in with his girlfriend and live in this big house by the end of the summer.*" From what I heard of the conversation I knew he was referring to me. That's when I realized he was as crazy as a betsy bug! This guy was downright looney-tune! So although I wasn't even dating him, I had to throw him back!

CARMINE

The next *LEECH* would be Carmine. This was a 36-year-old man who my friend bugged me for months to meet. When I *finally* said ok, I was immediately set up to deal with another *LEECH*. He seemed nice enough and I ended up hanging out with him a handful of times. However, as I got to know him more, the *LEECH* characteristics began to reveal themselves!

I realized he lived in a townhouse with his brother, with no motivation or plan of owning a place of his own. He had a yard the size of an average person's bathroom and yet was too lazy to mow it himself. He actually hired someone to do it. I would invite him over to hang out, and he didn't seem to know when to leave.

After hanging out with him for several weeks, Carmine threw out a comment that stunned me. He said something to the effect of: "*Now, I don't want to rush into anything, but maybe I could move in with you by the end of the summer.*" This statement was made in May. I met him in April... of the same year! "*I could pay you like $500 or maybe $700 towards the mortgage a month, and we could see how things go with us.*"

I realized right then, Carmine was not only a **LEECH**, but also a little crazy like the last guy. I lived in a brand new construction home that was 3,100 square feet and this guy, at 36 years old, thought he could pay me a few hundred bucks a month to live with me?!?! Not to mention I had known him for all of three weeks! Can you say, crazy- **LEECH**?!?!?!?? I think you know what's coming next. I threw him back!

JACE

Jace was a young guy in his early twenties. He was fun, charismatic, and always cracking jokes. When I first met him, I would talk to him on the phone for hours at a time— literally. This was fun, maybe for the first week I knew him, but it got old really fast. Especially when I would tell him over and over again, "*Ummm I have to get up at 5:30 AM for work. I need to get off of the phone so I can go to bed.*" His response was always the same, "*Oh ok, no problem. I'll let you go right after I tell you one more story.*" Then an hour later he would still be talking. After several weeks of this I finally started to say to him, "*Jace, just stop talking. I'm hanging up the phone because I told you I have to go. So please stop talking and say goodbye.*" His response? "*Heeeyyyy, that wasn't very nice to tell me to stop talking.*" Then he would immediately continue to tell whatever story he was droning on about.

He was also the kind of person who would over-welcome his stay, to the point where I started to hope some crazy disaster would happen in a nearby neighborhood that would prompt the police to come to evacuate all of the houses.

In addition, this guy would literally eat me out of house and home. He would eat *everything*! He was like an animal! I am not a soda drinker, but I would sometimes keep a variety of sodas in my refrigerator so I had something other than just water to offer my guests. He would drink them *all*!

Not only would he consume everything in sight, he never cleaned up after himself. There would be piles of crumbs, spilled soda, empty soda cans everywhere, empty or half-filled glasses of water bottles, in my living room and on my kitchen countertops. There would be residue from cheese, grease or mayonnaise all over the counters or kitchen table… EVERYWHERE! My place was a disgusting mess when he came over! I felt like I was constantly cleaning up after him.

Now I do have to give this guy credit where some credit is due. I confronted him about eating me out of house and home and told him I couldn't possibly afford to continue in this manner. I told him it was pretty disrespectful to be a guest in my home and behave in that manner, and that he was taking advantage of my hospitality. He did apologize in a way that seemed very genuine. Later that same night he gave me over $200.00 in cash to help make up for the cost of all of the groceries he ate. Little did he know he ate and drank close to $700.00 worth, but the guy did try.

The "talking to," didn't stop him from sucking all of the energy from me when we were together or even just on the phone. It was like having a fulltime job when associated with him. He just demanded *so much attention*!!! So… I threw him back.

RAFAEL

My friend **Liza** had a *LEECH* she knew she had to throw back, **Rafael**, but was very reluctant to do so. They had known each other for ages and had become a bit of a habit. She moved away, far away, to help her do so, but still couldn't quite cut the line. He, on the other hand, was going to hang on for as long as possible. And why wouldn't he? She flew him to visit her in exotic places and any time they went out, he'd up and leave so she'd have to the bill! He was very rude and insensitive and the stories about this *LEECH* are bountiful, but they are only the precursor to one of the most outrageous date stories!

Before I get into the story I need to put out a disclaimer. I in no way advocate our behavior. There are better ways to de-*LEECH*. Liza and I were inconsiderate and should've handled things better than we did, but unfortunately it didn't go down that way.

Liza was making a sincere effort to get over Rafael and my friends and I thought we better support her in her efforts. Given I was the only single one of the bunch, I had to take one for the team and accompany Liza on a double date. Liza had met the bachelors a week or so prior to our date and she said they seemed to be nice and hot. Well, she must have been viewing through some pretty heavy beer goggles because they were far from hot OR interesting!

Not only did they arrive late and kept us waiting for thirty minutes, but when we made it to the fantastic little Paella restaurant that Liza and I adored, they also began to bash it because it was a gay-friendly place! Needless to say, the conversation was strained. Although we put our best feet forward, our patience was wearing thin. However, in the spirit of supporting Liza in her efforts to throw Rafael back, I tried to stick it out as long as I could.

It was clear we were feeling the same way because when we went to the powder room we instantly began to figure out a way to run for the hills. And we meant to **run**. We were so serious about it we even considered exiting through the open window in the bathroom, but since the drop to the bottom was too steep, we returned to our seats.

The guys suggested we head to a Latin American bar to dance, but what they didn't tell us was they didn't know how to salsa! There we were in a crowded bar, with a bunch of Latin Americans with some suave dance moves, with two guys who kept stepping on our toes and elbowing the other dancers left and right! The date started off bad, but it had quickly gone from worse to worse than worse again!!

We decided to head to the bathroom again, but encountered the same problem! No exit! We then concocted a plan...we needed a red herring and decided that we'd head to this little bar called, "Toro" because it had two levels. If we lured the guys to the bottom floor, in time we would have to make it to the restrooms, which were on the first floor, and then we could high-tail it out of there.

It worked and as soon as we got to the first floor we RAN out of the club and into the streets...and once we were in the streets, we couldn't get away quickly enough and we kept running! We even jumped into a taxi to get as far as possible, as fast as possible!

Unfortunately, the experience discouraged Liza and about a week or so later Rafael was visiting again. We all went to that Paella place and ran into the guys we ditched!! We all pretended not to know one another!

Ladies if your friend is dating a *LEECH* you've got to take one for the team! Just be SURE you don't exchange a *LEECH* for some other *THROW BACK*!!!

Are you being sucked dry? Review the *LEECH* characteristics below!

☐ His philosophy is: What's yours is mine – and- what's mine is mine.

☐ He spends *your* money like it grows on trees.

☐ He mistakes your kitchen pantry for a COSTCO.

☐ He tries to monopolize your time and doesn't understand why you'd spend one moment without him.

Ok, so you're being sucked dry… You know what to do…pry him off of the hook and THROW HIM BACK!

THE GEFILTE FISH

THE OBSESSIVE-COMPULSIVE LOVER OF HIS OWN ETHNICITY

THIS FISH COMES FROM A FAMILY where everyone is of one strong, ethnic culture. They always talk about being this ethnicity and they socialize only with members of their culture. They incessantly emphasize the importance of their culture and marry their "own kind." They only eat traditional ethnic food. They think their country of origin is the only place in the world to go visit and vacation.

You may naively think you shouldn't judge this fish by how overbearing his family is— but you would be wrong. The school that the *GEFILTE FISH* comes from is a powerful bunch. They manipulate like the *SHARK* and wait for the opportunity to tear you to shreds like the *PIRANHA*. The school of fish the *GEFILTE FISH* was raised in, expect generation after generation of fish to be exactly the same as previous generations in terms of religion, beliefs, practices, cuisine, child rearing, and so on. There is no room for change and they refuse to accept that other people might have *their own belief system*—one different from theirs!

The older generations typically forbid their children to marry outside of their ethnic/religious network. For example, if you're Greek then you only marry Greeks or if you're Jewish you're only allowed to marry other Jewish people, Catholics with Catholics, and so on. If for some same strange reason a *GEFILTE FISH* offspring is dating a person who is not of the same ethnicity/religion, then that poor girlfriend is either "run off"— or— is expected to convert religions if she plans on sticking around. If she sticks around, she will be 'schooled' by other family members as to how their future children will be raised according to the cultural standards. Yep, the full cultural shebang.

The parents, and especially mothers of the *GEFILTE FISH*, are typically friendly, overly generous, loud and social on the outside, but get her alone and you'll find an extremely manipulative, sneaky, and controlling Mother fish!

What makes a guy fall into the category of a *GEFILTE FISH* is if he and/or his family are not open to embracing other people outside of their own cultural circle. A lot of the time, the severity of the control that these parents have over their kids isn't fully realized until after a marriage commitment has been made.

I hate to be the bearer of bad news, but if you're with a *GEFILTE FISH*, then you're most likely headed for a life of torment. This is not the kind of family who is open to different cultures and religions and respects *your* beliefs for what they are. They will not merge your belief system into theirs. They expect you to practice what they preach and there is no acceptance of having things any other way. Compromise does not exist, except that you will compromise your way of doing things to practice theirs.

So why should you throw back a *GEFILTE FISH?* Because life is too damn short to put up with crazy people! There are enough stressors in life then to have to put up with people trying to control how you cook, what you eat, what you believe in, what place of worship you go to and how often, what type of clothes you wear, how you raise your kids, how to fold your towels, where to put your belongings and organize your kitchen… I *could* go on, but you get the picture!

The bottom line? You are just as important as the person you choose to spend the rest of your life with. Your beliefs, customs, religion, and culture are JUST AS VALUABLE as your significant other's. So don't you dare allow him (or worse yet, his family members) to force you to take a back seat to your own traditions or customs. If this is happening, then urgent steps to change this are essential. Unfortunately, in many of these strong, ethnic cultures, change is extremely unlikely. You will be labeled by the family as the "black-sheep," if you attempt to stray outside of their traditions and there *will be consequences* to non-conformity!

The truth is, even if his family is being prejudice, biased and controlling, the *GEFILTE FISH* has been brainwashed his entire life to listen to these very family members without disagreeing. He will always feel torn and put in the middle. It's very important to know that the *GEFILTE FISH* lacks the gumption to stand up to their family members (especially their mothers) no matter how unfair, inappropriate, disrespectful, or even *crazy* their/her behaviors are. In the end, the person who always loses is **_you_**.

If the *GEFILTE FISH* or his family can't accept and respect you for who you are, then you need to throw him back and find a better quality fish with a more loving and accommodating family. Although this may be very difficult to do, you will be so much better off in the long run because he will <u>always</u> *pick them over you*. It goes against the very nature of his being to do otherwise.

If you yourself come from a *GEFILTE FISH* family, another *GEFILTE FISH* might gain automatic acceptance by your family members, whether he is good for you or not. That is, by virtue of being "culture x" your family might weigh that criteria against all others. Be weary and advocate for yourself. If he is not right for you, simply having the same culture/ethnicity doesn't automatically make him a good **catch**. A *THROW BACK* is a *THROW BACK* is a *THROW BACK*!

JARED

I met **Jared** through a friend of mine; he was an attractive guy with bright blue eyes and curly locks. I don't even know how we ended up dating, considering the fact he was bound and determined to be serious only with Jewish women and I was of Christian background!

I remember the first time we met. A friend invited us over to her house for dinner. She is a great cook and I'd never skip an invite to her house. We were joined by another neighbor for pasta with eggplant and feta. I still remember the dish to this day! That very weekend we all ended up having breakfast and somehow things took off from there.

Jared hooked me and we wound up spending a lot of time together! We even ended up taking a weekend trip together. However, for as much as he was drawn toward me, he was also repelled because I wasn't Jewish. For me it wasn't an issue because I had been exposed to a number of bi-religious and bi-cultural marriages whose family members embraced each other and respected the merging family. In my experience those families adopted their own traditions, practices and perspectives, and for them culture and religion took on a novel, innovative and new form unique to the merged family. Therefore, from my perspective I was shocked when Jared, the man who had pursued me, told me he'd have to throw <u>me</u> back!

I was so hurt by this! This guy had come on to me! He had initiated everything! Why would he do that when he knew from DAY ONE he would only become serious with a Jewish woman and I was <u>not</u> Jewish?! How could he overlook the fun we had had and the dynamic that put us in the predicament of having to evaluate our time together in the first place?!

This was a hard blow that stung for quite a while. I just couldn't wrap my mind around why someone would make the choices he made and walk away from it as if he had done nothing wrong. Not only that, but this coming from a guy who didn't want me to eat a bacon and cheese potato in front of him, but he could have pepperoni pizza and bacon burgers when he needed comfort food. Yes, it was clear he was a conflicted soul.

Anyway, the point here is that if you meet a guy who won't accept you as you are, or who ignores the dynamic you have because you're not up to par, he is a *THROW BACK*. Do not get hooked, and if you're the one fishing, put down the pole and find another fishing hole.

KIMBERLY'S GEFILTE FISH

Kimberly was fishing after being dealt a low blow by her ex fiancé, a Slippery Dick (you'll read about those later!). She was a gorgeous and talented woman who *knows* she deserves the best and was not about to settle for less. A little green around the gills, but ready nonetheless, she joined the thousands of people in the online dating world… and wound up meeting a *GEFILTE FISH*.

Kimberly's story was a lot like the Jared story. Two people met, they hit it off really well, and then just when things started to heat up, he told her that anything more would be impossible.

"*Sounds like a GEFILTE FISH to me,*" I told her. I warned her there was no future and bet her he'd suggest a conversion in order for him to even consider a commitment. Well, the scenario played out to a T.

They had a whale of time hanging out, getting together, traveling, and spending virtually every non-working moment together! He wanted all the benefits and none of the responsibility! Since things were heating up, he asked her if she would convert and move back to the Mother Land with him.

It was to the point where Kimberly knew the fun had ended and it was indeed time to throw him back. She looked at him and *knew* the wait was over. She was done and was not going to allow this *GEFILTE FISH* to steal any more of her valuable time. She grabbed her pole and went 'fishin!' in more welcoming waters.

Did you reel in a *GEFILTE FISH*? Remember this is what they're like!

☐ You are one in their crowd with little or no identity.

☐ Sharing your own traditions and cultural practices is not a possibility.

☐ You do things their way or no way at all.

☐ Compromise = doing it their way.

☐ Holidays—well there are no other holidays than the ones they celebrate, right?

☐ Vacations—Why wouldn't you want to spend every single one of them with the extended family or in a remote village in the "homeland?"

☐ Conversion is a must because there is no room for "other" here.

☐ You're expected to spend your honeymoon with other members of the family.

☐ No one tries the dish you prepared for the holiday meal because it's not "their" type of food.

Take action! Cut the line! Throw him back!!! You have a right to accept, cherish, value and take pleasure in your cultural norms too! If you're not in a network that embraces that... FIND a network that will!!! Remember—you shouldn't make a fish a priority, if he really isn't even an option!!

THE RAINBOW FISH

THE CLOSET GAY

EVER BEEN ON A DATE with a guy whose clothing, physique, mannerisms, and the pitch of his voice scream "I'm gay," but the first thing out of his mouth comes the declaration that he's straight?

BEAU

It all started after a few disappointing date-a-paloozas. You know, the kind where you sit at the table with your drink, sitting one out because the dude so desperate for a companion shows up late and throws off the entire schedule. But it doesn't end there because when he does arrive he drops a monologue on how his car broke down and he's hurtin' for work so if you could "send him work that would be great". Whoa buddy, I'd like to throw you back *before* they ring that bell!

Or the one where the age cut off was between 32 and 42 and the sixty-something's show up?! The ones who are too old to date *your mother*, let alone *you*.

Well, I was feeling the backlash of the speed-dating scene when the girls decided to get involved.

Mary was at work and wound up making contact with a single guy who rescues dogs. Given I'm a dog lover, and that my dog is a rescue, she thought we'd at least have one point of common interest. She sent the link to my webpage, and sent me the link to his rescue site. I checked out the pictures with Tamera and we decided to give it a thumbs-up. The pictures were all right, the cause was noble, and the website suggested a guy with substance. So, we set up a date!

We met at a little Thai restaurant with a brilliant array of curries. It was a favorite place of mine and a very nice date spot. It also promised the food would be good, even if the date went sour, so it was a winner.

Beau arrived on time, so we were off to a good start. He spotted me and made his way to the table. We introduced ourselves and it was as if a record skipped. As soon as he opened his mouth *I knew* this date was going to be a disaster! The first words out of his mouth were, "*I'm not gay.*"

Beau began to talk about his rescues. He spoke of the abuses they suffered, the sweetness of his dogs, and how well they've been integrated into families with children, cats and other pets. At this point the conversation was pretty normal...until suddenly he broke into tears and began to **wail** about the dogs. I'm all for men being in tune with their feelings and certainly don't believe a cryin' man is half a man (as the song goes). But this was our first date and the guy was a sobbing mess at the table! Ok, he's passionate I get it. These dogs have suffered and I get that too, but an all-out CRY on the first date?!

Once Beau composed himself and wiped away his tears, he took notice of my cute little Ecuadorian sweater-coat, and commented on it. YES! *Wait for it...* are you ready? Brace yourself because he actually said...

"Ohhhh my God! That sweater is soooo cute, hun. Those pom poms just make the outfit! What a great little find!"

Now, no straight man would ever say something like that, nor would a straight man think the pom poms made the outfit. A straight man doesn't even know what a pom pom is! *I* didn't even *like* the pom poms, but didn't want to cut them off so soon after buying the sweater!

Needless to say I did not see Beau again.

After the date I called Tamera and asked her why Mary tried to set me up with a closet gay. She joked with me saying she thought he was gay from his website, but decided not to say anything because it was unfair to judge a book by its cover. She also went on to tell me that Beau's famous first words, "I'm not gay," were *also* his first words when he had met Mary and her friends!!! Naïve Mary threw her intuition out the window and chose to believe the guy even though he hadn't convinced one other person in the room that he was straight! To top it, off she still tried to set me up with him. I've not gone on another date that had Mary's seal of approval.

Todd

I met Todd out one night, after seeing a famous stand-up comic with a friend. He was very handsome, muscular, extremely masculine, and had beautiful chocolaty skin. Oh, and he was also in the military. We started dating and getting to know him was exciting and fun. He was chivalrous and charming, quite the gentlemen. I did start to wonder why we had hung out several times and he hadn't even kissed me yet. Maybe he was really trying to hit the gentlemen thing home. He did finally give me a first kiss after a handful of dates. Boy was it delightful! His full lips felt so soft against mine and I couldn't wait for our next hang out so he could kiss me again!

In the meantime, I noticed he would always bring up homosexuality. Funny, he would somehow weave it into every conversation. He admitted he didn't like it about himself, but he was homophobic. He also stated that someone he knew his entire life came out of the closet a couple years back, and since then he was trying to eliminate his homophobia.

We continued dating. He always made future plans to hang out again before ending the night. But there was one problem, he had only kissed me that one time, and he continued to bring up the topic of gay men. When we were apart, he would text me flirtations that were sexual in nature, and he would frequently tell me I had the most incredible body he had ever seen. But he would make absolutely no sexual advances towards me when we were in person. Then he started showing me images of gay men on his phone. He would play it off like it was by accident… that somehow some naked man mysteriously showed up in his photos without him knowing how it got there. One night he came to hang out at my house with me. We were lying on the couch together watching a movie. He started telling me about a movie he was watching at home and to his disgust and surprise there was a gay sex scene. He proceeded to play this scene for me on his phone where he had saved it. He didn't just quickly show me either, he let the seven-minute, sex in all different positions, different angles and the shower scene play, even after I showed clear disinterest. Now I admit it took me about thirty seconds to show disinterest, but for six-in-a-half minutes I had turned away and went back to watching the movie that he came over to watch with me. For those six-and-a-half minutes, all I could think was, "Ok! Enough is enough! You are clearly gay, in the closet with no hope of coming out while you're in the military!"

Now I do think this guy would be an unbelievable catch for a gay man, but Christ Almighty! I could've been out, one step closer to meeting my Big Tuna and not wasting my time with this guy! If he had been honest from the beginning, I would have loved to hang out with him as friends. He really could have made a great buddy, but after pretending to be something he wasn't, no thank you!

Let's get something straight or rather *clear*. We believe strongly in human rights, including gay rights. No one here on any level is against homosexuality. What we are against, are those that are gay who choose to hide behind dating the opposite sex. It's not a truthful, virtuous way to live when you could entangle or hurt another person by your lack of honesty.

So how do you know if the man you're with is a *RAINBOW FISH*?

☐ One of the first things he says when he meets you is, "I'm not gay."

☐ He not only knows what the pom poms are on your sweater, but he squeals with delight when he sees them.

☐ He'll only have anal sex with you.

☐ He claims to be homophobic because it prevents you from thinking *he's* gay.

☐ *Your intuition* tells you he is suppressing his homosexuality.

☐ He says he's willing to "take one for the team" and watch gay porn if it will turn you on.

☐ He tripped and his penis ended up in the anus of a man.

☐ This one will definitey never send you a dick pic.

CATFISH

I'm Not Who I Say I Am

THE URBAN DICTIONARY DEFINES a catfish as someone who creates a false identity in social networks for the purpose of pursuing deceptive romantic relationships. The picture these kind of people paint of themselves, are a façade and are often **grossly different** than who they are in reality. They play with the affections of the people they're deceiving, reel them in, and take advantage of their vulnerabilities, their desire to connect with someone, their need to love and be loved, and exploit them for the fun of it. They have to be the scummiest of all the fish because they do this KNOWINGLY. They make a choice to deceive. They find a victim and outline a plan of attack and then put that plan into action. There's an entire show dedicated to the hurt that these bottom feeders cause!

Let's have a look at what's happening here. How can someone fall in love with someone they've never met? How can someone believe a relationship can be built off of internet chats, text messages, email, and phone calls alone? How do people fall victim to the predatory *CATFISH*?!

Well, we all just want to be loved and we all seek acceptance and companionship. The healthiest and happiest people on the planet are people who have a sense of belonging and who are a part of a community where they not only feel supported, but also needed. A community where they support and are supported by the group, and where there's reciprocity in terms of give and take, support and nurturing, responsibility and independence. There's a saying that describes this dynamic precisely and beautifully:

The strength of the wolf is the pack; the strength of the pack is the wolf.

For many of us today, the pathway to such a community is through our primary relationship; that is, the person with whom we are committed and connected. We have a great need as human beings for such a connection, a need so great, that we can become catfish prey. So, how do we get what we want and avoid being skinned by a Catfish?

We have to understand INTIMACY. Intimacy implies being known. True romantic intimacy, requires two people take the time to get to know one another on an emotional level, an experiential level, intellectually, and physically all while being completely vulnerable to one another. However, knowing one another requires good communication skills, honesty and transparency, vulnerability, and reciprocity. What does this look like? We call it the FOUR SEASONS.

A couple gets to know one another over time. They begin to spend time together and discover they have similar interests and values. They begin to share with one another on an emotional level and what they do, what they talk about, how they talk, begins to dive into topics that you don't (or wouldn't) share with others. As they take the time to get to know one another and they spend more time together, each person becomes central to the other. Relationships of secondary importance take their natural place as the couple form the relationship of primary importance with one another. This begins to lead to physical closeness, and over time, to romance.

Many people jump the gun on this! So many people struggle with boundaries and jump in too quickly, or share too much too soon, or mistake believing that intimacy is being created when it is not. Intimacy takes time, and not everyone is worthy of it! Some people just want their ego stroked and when a person of secondary or tertiary importance pays attention to them, they think there's more there than there actually is. Have you ever heard people calling someone they just met their FRIEND? That term is used so loosely! Many people's *friends* are really just acquaintances. This same mistake can happen with intimacy as well.

Now we need to digress a little bit here. We've referred to intimacy numerous times. Most people don't have a clue what true intimacy in a relationship actually is. The average person's understanding of what intimacy is tends to be superficial. Being truly intimate with a person doesn't mean just physical or sexual closeness. Intimacy can only develop when you have no walls up, your guard is down, and you're honest, virtuous and transparent with your actions. People can be married to each other for years and not have true intimacy with their partners. Just because you love or care for someone, by no means automatically leads to true intimacy between the two of you. You need to first be aware of what genuine intimacy is, (vs. closeness or the feeling of love) and then you need to do the work on yourself to offer and then to receive that level of deep bonding with another person. No relationship can ever be truly wonderful, truly magical, or filled with everlasting love, if there isn't a genuine level of true intimacy. It is important enough that we could write an entire other book on the subject. Since that is not the sole focus of this book, we encourage seeking out and beginning to learn and practice true intimacy in your relationships with other people. In the meantime, the following are some examples of intimacy and can be used as goals for yourself so you can better your relationships in the future.

True Intimacy is:

100% transparency, no text message, email, phone conversation or anything else is kept hidden or withheld from your partner.

Even when you have fears, you share openly with your partner. Facing your fears together is a way to create true emotional intimacy and strengthen your bond with one another.

If your partner 'checks up on you' (out of loving curiosity and the desire to be included, NOT out of jealousy or lack of trust), you should feel appreciative and are opened up. You are grateful your partner cares enough to be a part of the people you are engaged with.

You are completely vulnerable, raw, and exposed emotionally, for you realize this is the only path to develop actual intimacy and not just a superficial closeness with someone.

When you have a disagreement no defensiveness comes as a reaction, only caring concern with how to lovingly mend the conflict.

You listen with the intent to understand, not with the intent to reply.

You stop blaming others for your unhappiness and you instead turn within and work on you.

Your choices, actions and reactions in your relationship are not guided or driven by fear, only by love.

You remain intimate, loving, vulnerable, and open despite what any person has done to hurt you. You don't wish them ill will or harm. You understand they are on their individual path and will learn their own lessons in time. You do not settle or become a doormat, but you also do not allow yourself to harden, blame, or allow the walls to prevent intimacy to build just because another person wasn't ready for an intimate and loving relationship.

When you take the time to get to know another person, you give yourself the chance to see how they handle the ups and downs of life. Do they handle what life throws at them with grace and dignity? Or are they a monstrous mess? How do they respond to the ups and downs that life throws at you? Do they act in a loving and supporting way? Are they there for you in terms of real action or do they pay lip service? How your catch handles adversity is a huge indicator of his emotional, psychological, and spiritual condition and this is impossible to observe virtually. For this, there IS NO VIRTUAL REALITY. There is no chance to develop true intimacy with a person, if there is physical distance between you, especially at the 'getting to know you' phase. There is no substitute for real time spent in the presence of the catch, live and in the flesh. Without that, you're fooling yourself, or worse, you're letting yourself get CATFISHED!

The *CATFISH*:

☐ Someone 'falling in love' with you even though they have never met you.

☐ You need to pay for their plane ticket in order for them to come see you.

☐ He always wants you to drive everywhere.

☐ You go out to dinner and they forgot their wallet.

☐ You barely know him, but he wants to marry you.

☐ He doesn't have a green card.

☐ You get a call to bail him out of jail.

☐ He always gives a vague answer about what he does for a living.

SLIPPERY DICK

THE CHEATER

YES WE ALL KNOW THIS KIND; the guy whose penis is so slippery it slides into places it just shouldn't go. This is the kind of guy who likes to have a girlfriend/fiancé/wife on his arm, but still likes to act like a **DOG FISH** or even a **SHARK** when his significant other is not around. Somehow if a female did actually throw herself at or on him (like the **SLIPPERY DICK** always claims), he'll claim to have done everything in his power to stop her advances. Strangely, this magical force seems to take hold of his penis and renders him helpless— like kryptonite to superman—and no matter what actually transpires, 1st, 2nd, 3rd base, or even a homerun, this **SLIPPERY DICK** cannot possibly be held responsible for his actions.

This is the same guy who acts in a suspicious or untrusting manner and then harps on you for asking questions, or looking at his cell phone to see who he is communicating with, or even looking at his email. Remember, people who have nothing to hide, hide nothing. I repeat: PEOPLE WHO HAVE NOTHING TO HIDE, HIDE NOTHING.

Now, a healthy loving relationship shouldn't be filled with people constantly 'checking up' on the other one. There shouldn't be a need for that. What I'm saying is if the person you are committed to *is* acting suspiciously and your instincts keep telling you something is wrong, *then* you have every right to investigate. A man, who acts defensively or turns the tables on you and claims you are "crazy" or you're "a snoop," is clearly telling you, he is in fact a *SLIPPERY DICK*. A mature, nurturing response from someone who has nothing to hide should be an open-book about every aspect of his life. It just shouldn't be a big deal unless he has something to hide.

Let's face it, if you have a lack of trust in your relationship, you need to immediately address it to properly work things out or you need to get out of the relationship. Feeling like you can't trust someone is a 'slippery slope' to disaster.

It is also important to remember, that just because you have been lied to or cheated on in the past, doesn't give you the right to automatically label the next guy as a *SLIPPERY DICK, Dog Fish* or any other type of *THROW BACK*. If you do this, then you're dooming your relationship before it even starts. If you can't let go of what someone else did to you in the past, then you are clearly not ready to be in a relationship. You need to do whatever it takes to truly deal with whatever hurt feelings you have, and then let it go. You need to do this as a SINGLE woman, otherwise you will attract all the *DOG FISH, SHARK*s, and *SLIPPERY DICK*s out there! Work on healing yourself so your Big **Tuna** can be attracted into your life.

TREVHOR

Once a *SLIPPERY DICK*, always a *SLIPPERY DICK*. **Trevhor** and Angeline dated for about three years. Trevhor was a few years older than Angeline and had already begun college when the two met. Angeline was studious and a bit of a book worm and was naturally more drawn to a college guy than a high-schooler. She made a poor choice because this college student was spending a bit of his free time back home, rather than with his college buddies.

At first it worked because the two got to spend a lot of time together. But what Angeline didn't know was after they'd say their goodbyes, Trevhor used to go out to the local high school parties and let loose. Of course he was surrounding himself with *BLOWFISH,* (see chapter on *BLOWFISH*) who would not blow his *cover* and so it took well into the third year before Angeline found out the depth of the lies and deception.

When the truth came to light Angeline moved on, but because she and Trevhor had a number of friends in common she would hear stories of Trevhor's improprieties. After the two broke up, Trevhor immediately began to date Crista. The two were "together" for seven years before they got married. Unfortunately for Crista, she still married him after she had caught him cheating more times than she could count! She was fully aware he was a *SLIPPERY DICK,* but she married him anyway! After two years –she threw him back and their divorce has finalized.

The stories of Trevhor's *SLIPPERY DICK* excursions, seemed completely and utterly farfetched, but they were true nonetheless. I mean, a girl he barely knew, once bit him, so hard she drew blood! Try explaining that one.

Jake

About a year after college, Rebecca met up with a friend who had moved to Philadephia. She had a boyfriend, and her boyfriend had a roommate. Now Angie began telling Rebecca about the roommate Jake and how incredible he was. She was determined to set up Jake and Rebecca. Ironically they all ended up at the same bar one evening, totally unplanned. Jake laid eyes on Rebecca and immediately told his friends to look at the beautiful blonde across the room. Angie almost had a heart attack, "that's Rebecca!! The one I've been telling you about!" Well Rebecca finally met Jake and they hit it off immediately.

They began dating and spending a lot of time together, time that was intoxicating. Jake was a blonde, extremely fit, and a muscular, spiky haired scientist. Try that for an interesting combination. Jake and Rebecca clicked and formed a strong connection right away. The best part was that a genuine and very strong friendship was developing between the two of them. It wasn't just a superficial romantic dating experience. However, Rebecca noticed the occasional phone call Jake would ignore and then eventually, strategically leave the room. He also had a pattern of going home to his parents' house almost every other weekend. It was a little strange for a 25 year old to go to his parents' and spend the weekend on a fairly regular basis. This was about an hour away from where he lived in Philly. Rebecca's intuition told her something wasn't right, but she couldn't find any real proof that he wasn't trustworthy. Of course, when questioned, he always had 'logical reason' for going home frequently. When they spent their first Christmas exchanging gifts, Rebecca dismissed her intuition and assumed for some reason she was just being paranoid. Then there she was, in the mall with her friend and roommate Jimmy, doing last minute Christmas shopping together, when they saw what made Rebecca's heart stop in her chest, move to her throat and almost suffocate her. There was Jake, walking arm in arm with his girlfriend.

Rebecca got together with him in an attempt to find out the truth.

It turns out he had a very long time girlfriend that lived "back home." Jake's explanation was that he met Rebecca and quickly fell head-over-heals in love with her. He had been dragging out his relationship with his high school sweetheart for a very long time. He was too scared to end it, because he cared about her so much. However, according to him, she never went to college and didn't seem to have much direction in life. He was no longer in love with her and knew with 100% certainty that he was not going to marry her or be with her in the future. But he didn't have the balls to end things with her. Instead he tried spending less and less time with her, kind of hoping she would break up with him. What a coward.

Rebecca has ALWAYS lived by the motto to NEVER fight over the catch. Rebecca is NOT a woman who knowingly enters any relationship with a man who is taken. She believes women should look out for each other, not betray one another. ALL women should hold men accountable, so she ended things with Jake immediately, never to look back. It certainly wasn't easy because she was on the road to falling in love with Jake. It made things more painful when he sent messages, e-cards, phone calls, etc. exclaiming how he missed her and wanted his best friend back. It made Rebecca cry every time, but he had shown his true colors. That was where he was in his life, a place of dishonesty. No matter the temporary pain it caused, Rebecca would not settle for a *SLIPPERY DICK*.

The most profound thing was Angie knew Jake had a girlfriend the entire time and she was a part of the lies. She knew his story and sympathized with him, viewing him as someone who just needed a good woman so he'd have the courage to finally end it with his high school sweetheart. CALLING ALL WOMEN! CALLING ALL WOMEN! WAKE THE HELL UP! How dysfunctional must your thinking be to encourage and participate in that?! We are supposed to look out for one another, not knowingly put each other in painful, egocentric, drama-filled situations! Angie had just as much to learn in the scenario as Jake did. Needless to say, Rebecca cut the line with Angie just as cleanly as she did with Jake.

Ladies, if you come to find that you are committed to a '*SLIPPERY DICK*,' then you better tie an anchor to his fins, throw him back, and race to shore never to look back! Once he realizes he can cheat on you and you'll forgive him for it, he will automatically lose respect for you. He then knows he can continue to do it and if caught, still get away with it. Trust your intuition, if you suspect something fishy is going on, it probably is. Let him slip away! Let that slimy bastard slither into the depth of the cold murky waters where he belongs! If he cheats on you once shame on *him*, if you don't throw him back and he cheats again, shame on *you*.

The SLIPPERY DICK:

☐ Blames other people for the situations he ends up in.

☐ Doesn't take responsibility for his actions.

☐ He always justifies cheating.

☐ Has mysterious bite-marks (or genital critters), but he *"never cheated."*

☐ Never apologizes or admits wrong doing.

☐ Doesn't answer his cell phone.

☐ Has an excuse for his whereabouts.

☐ Has plenty of time that he can't account for.

☐ Claims to not remember what happened…or who he was with.

☐ Puts you on the defensive for questioning the various situations.

☐ Smells like perfume or sex.

☐ *If* he apologizes for his behavior, he expects you to *just get over it.*

☐ Suppresses information and/or questions so he doesn't have to provide information he doesn't want you to know.

☐ Disappears or spends a lot of alone time when he's not in much contact with you.

☐ Has 1001 dick pics in the Security File App on his phone.

FIREMOUTH

THE JEALOUS, ABUSIVE CONTROL FREAK

FIREMOUTHS TEND to be jealous, possibly depressed, controlling men who isolate women from friends, family and loved ones. They tend to try to intimidate and make threats making their mate feel vulnerable, weak, helpless or defenseless. Whatever the form – abuse is abuse and should NOT be tolerated. Life with a *FIREMOUTH* is an inferno and anyone involved with this kind of fish will sink deeper and deeper into the depths of agony, anguish, and misery. Oftentimes they'll declare their sorrow and vow to change, but their patterns **will be repeated**. No matter what it takes, no matter how tight the grip, THIS FISH IS A *THROW BACK*. Do whatever it takes to throw him back! Consult Women's Resource Centers, the National Domestic Abuse Hotline, Counseling of Mental Health Centers, your doctor, or local law enforcement. We are only trying to alert you to potential abusive situations, if you need assistance please be sure to consult the proper channels for help.

MARIAH'S FIREMOUTH

I met Mariah in college, she was a delightful little thing and when she smiled her whole face lit up. When she met and started dating Seth, I thought it was a little strange he didn't want to hang out in a group. Mariah said it was because he was a couple of years older and therefore "more mature and wanted to spend quality time with her to get to know her." What wasn't realized at the time was that this was his way of beginning to isolate her from her friends. Over a period of a year or more, we saw less and less of Mariah and when she did go out with the girls, he would make her feel guilty. He'd beg her not to go, and sometimes even cry telling her that he loved her so much and was only trying to protect her from anything bad happening to her. I also noticed that Mariah's personality was changing through this process of isolation. She started to isolate herself more. What was so astounding to me was that many of our friends seemed to be oblivious.

One night, in which she actually did go out with us, she disappeared within an hour of arriving at the party. I thought she had just gone to the bathroom, but she was nowhere to be found! She didn't come back to the dorm that night. No phone calls. No messages. Nothing. No one heard anything until the next morning when she showed up pounding on my door. When I let her in, she told me a terrifying story. Seth had shown up at the party, saw her entering the bathroom, grabbed her wrists and dragged her outside. She was so petrified that when an acquaintance asked her if she was ok she responded with, "Yeah, fine. I'll see ya tomorrow." Seth pulled her into the woods behind where his car was parked and raped her. Then he took her to his apartment, told her he loved her, and if she hadn't gone out to begin with, none of that would have happened.

I immediately called hotlines and provided Mariah with resources. I even offered to accompany her to campus counseling. While we were making these appointments, Seth showed up at my door, saying he wanted to see Mariah immediately, to be sure she wasn't telling me anything she wasn't supposed to be. I smiled at him and calmly told him to get the fuck away from me before I called the police. He leaned in close to me and whispered, "Be careful, or I'll do to you what I did to her." Since abusers like to intimidate by keeping things secret, I immediately started screaming at the top of my lungs, "Did you just threaten me?!?! Did you just fucking threaten me?!" By that time, close to twenty people or so were beginning to crowd the hallway. I continued in front of the witnesses, "Newsflash, dickhead, there are at least sixteen witnesses here who just heard you threaten me! I'm calling security and you'd better get the fuck away from me." I called campus security and got him banned from our dorm.

Although Mariah seemed as though she was on the right track by starting counseling, she soon fell prey to Seth's nonstop advances (roses, cards, love letters, etc.) Once he won her back she was forbidden to associate with me anymore. That was ok because I had stuck my neck out to help her. However, Mariah was the one who needed to do the throwing back. In the meantime, I made it clear that if she needed my support to throw him back, I'd be there to support, but for as long as she was with him I wouldn't be around in the name of my own safety. Once more, I was NOT going to be an enabler in this abusive relationship. Unfortunately, Mariah stayed with Seth for a few more years, but at some point she finally threw him back.

REED & LEAH

Reed was a FIREMOUTH who put Leah in the emergency room. Reed could turn angry in a flash; just about anything could set him off. When Leah would ask him how his day went he'd go into a rage and would bark that she was intrusive and controlling and had to know every little detail of his life. When Leah would tell a story, Reed would cut her off and remind her she need not be so dramatic in its retelling. When potential good news would come through the work pipeline, Leah was chastised for being happy over it or asking if Reed were excited about it because, after all, Reed didn't like the highs and lows of being excited about anything. When Leah quit asking about his day, or expressed confusion over Reed showing excitement over something, or quit sharing her stories with him, Reed was infuriated. He would call her the "ice queen" and comment on how distant she was being and how she was acting that way because she didn't want to see him happy.

All hell broke loose after a three-day argument about money. Leah had launched a side business that she planned to work in with some friends, in addition to her full-time job, as a way to make money and plan for the future. Reed wanted in on the action given that the business had tremendous revenue potential. The problem was it was a turnkey business, where only one owner could be named on the official paperwork. Since Reed's money was tied up in a business venture of his own, he didn't have the funds to be independently involved in the same biz as Leah. He said he would help Leah build up her business and build her wealth. He told her he would share contacts, work to build clients, and teach her what he knew about sales. The catch, however, was he wanted her to sign a document that stated he then was entitled to 50% of the profits of her business.

Leah had loaned Reed the start-up money for his side business. She had no such document stating she would be a fifty-percent holder in that endeavor, and given they only had a verbal agreement that he would re-pay her in full, Leah refused to a partnership merger for her side business until and unless Reed agreed to the same stipulations. Reed was furious and threatened not to help her in any way, shape, or form if she didn't sign. Leah told him he was an asshole and she could move forward on her own, reminding him that if he wanted to partake, she would sign a document that *leveled out the risk* and outlined stipulations for *all that was on the table.*

Reed was seething when he didn't get his way. He spent days picking fights and throwing tantrums. Leah did not back down, they fought ferociously. When Leah stood her ground for so long, Reed just snapped. He raised his fist at her and threatened to punch her.

"Oh, you're going to punch me? You're going to punch a woman?!"

"You'd better get the fuck out of here and just leave me alone before I do, you fucking bitch!"

"Well, you know what kind of men hit women, don't you? PUSSIES."

Reed shoved her forcefully out of the room and into the hallway doors as he told her what a bitch she was. He shoved her hard again further down the hall. Leah shoved him back and told him he crossed a line and had NO RIGHT to put a hand on her. She kicked him in the balls and stood her ground, bellowing that he had NO RIGHT to touch her. When she walked past him to try to get settled and dressed for work, he pounced on her from behind and took her down to the ground.

On the way down her face smashed first furniture and then the floor. He held her in a fight pose trying to dominate her and control her. Leah fought with every ounce of energy to get away. She dug into his side, but it did no good. She began to scratch and punch anything and everything she could to break the hold. Finally, she reached up and began to choke him – there was no way he could continue to hold her down if he couldn't breathe. It worked. Leah broke free, grabbed her belongings, texted a neighbor, and went running to the police for help.

Only, the police didn't help her, instead, they detained her due to the defensive wounds on Reed. "You're not hearing me," she pleaded. "He attacked me and I did everything I could to get away, and then I came to you for help." "You don't bear any such wounds," the officers said. "He smashed my head into the furniture and onto the floor, are you not hearing me?" "Oh, that little mark on your nose?" they asked snidely.

They weren't listening, it wasn't until they released her hours later that she was able to get help. As it turns out, she had a concussion and a broken nose. The police escorts she requested to accompany her to their apartment commented that she was slurring her speech and needed some rest. When she spoke to family members, people with backgrounds in the medical field, they recognized the signs of a concussion. They insisted she go to the nearest emergency room. She did and the doctors not only confirmed she had a concussion, but discovered that the "little mark on her nose," showed where her nose had been fractured. She was advised to follow up with her primary care doctor so they could not only evaluate her condition but also document the bruises that set in hours after the assault.

Reed stayed with friends for about a month to help things cool down, but there was about six weeks left on their lease after that. He did what abusers usually do – bought flowers, tried to be attentive and cooperative, made promises that things would get better, made grandiose declarations of love and commitment, begged her not to leave him, asked her to marry him and suggested they should get pregnant, and tried to convince Leah to change the story to paint him in a favorable light... such as... what happened was an accident – he was sleeping and didn't realize she had gotten out of bed and thought it was an intruder and blah, blah, blah.

Reed never told his friends what he did. His story was they got into a huge argument and needed some time apart for things to cool down. Another thing he never did was apologize. He never showed remorse or regret. Rather, he told her that she had to take responsibility for her part in what happened. *I mean, Leah never would have ended up with a concussion and a broken nose if she had just given him what he wanted –* and— *it was the neighbor's fault that Leah was detained because Reed knew better than to go to the authorities for help* — the sick and twisted reasoning of a FIREMOUTH.

Sydney & David

Sydney was allergic to bees and one sunny afternoon she was walking her dog in the park, when she noticed an unusually high number of hornets buzzing around. "I wonder if it's better to be in a skirt or if these jeans offer better protection," she pondered just as a hornet flew up her pant leg and began to bite her over and over.

Sydney hadn't been stung in over a decade or two and wasn't sure how this was going to play out, but she knew for sure that she had a life-threatening allergy. "Stay calm. Keep a clear mind and get to an Urgent Care Center *immediately*."

The park was peanut-shaped and she was at the far end of it, the farthest from her car. *Should I run through the middle, right through the hornets or just go along the track?* She first chose the track, petrified she might suffer more stings, but she could feel the effects of the six stings settling in and she knew she had to take the shorter route.

She made it to the car, but had two more obstacles: the heat and the traffic. Sydney couldn't leave the dog in a fiery hot car so she knew she had to get him home first and then pray the traffic would cooperate. Fortunately, it did and she made it to the Urgent Care Center before her throat closed completely.

In the UCC they gave Sydney the medicines and injections that saved her life, but she had to stay for observations for a minimum of one hour before they could release her. The good news was that her body was responding to the meds. The bad news was she wasn't going to be allowed to drive herself home and had to call David. She sent him a text explaining what had happened and that she needed him to get a ride to Urgent Care so he could drive her car home.

David rushed to the UCC sending text messages along the way. He was worried and growing frustrated when Sydney wasn't answering him. Frustrated?! Sydney was just injected with a cocktail meant to save her life, to keep her throat from closing and her body from shutting down, and David was getting pissed that his texts were being "ignored."

He burst into the Urgent Care Center and into Sydney's room right after the doctor had come for her evaluation. Sydney made him leave, she was exhausted and trying to process this near death experience. The last thing she needed was David in the room.

You're probably asking yourself why she felt that way? It seems like David cares and is responding like a **CATCH**, rather than a *THROWBACK*. Except that David was moody and had a temper – classic signs of a person with control issues. He had a way of making every situation about him and Sydney never knew how he was going to react. Given the circumstances, dealing with David's bullshit was the last thing she wanted to do after coming so close to losing her life. Dealing with his attitude about unanswered text messages while she was wondering if they got the meds in her system in time to prevent asphyxiation was not something she had the energy for.

By the time they got home Sydney was exhausted. She was on mega doses of steroids and antihistamines and was even more drained because she ended up having to drive home. David showed up with his car rather than follow the directions Sydney sent him. The garage wouldn't hold her car overnight and they wouldn't make concessions for the emergency either, so she ended up having to drive herself home anyway! David went back to work and Sydney went to sleep.

The next day, Sydney was relieved that there were no complications after her initial treatment and the meds were keeping her from worsening. Her throat was still half closed the next day, but it wasn't getting worse so everything pointed to her being out of the woods. She got up to take the dog for a walk around the block and to take in the beautiful day. She wanted to feel the sunlight on her face, to breathe the air *because she could breathe*, to watch her dog delight in the joys of his walk. She was grateful to have pulled through. She took a picture of a tree and posted it on the web, "what a beautiful day."

David called her as soon as he saw the post.

"What is wrong with you? Why would you post that picture? I told people we were cancelling our weekend with them because you got stung and weren't in a condition to make it and this picture makes it look like I'm lying."

"That picture and that caption make what happened look like a lie? How about it makes it look like I'm happy to be alive?!"

"You need to take it down. It makes me look bad."

SARAH & JOSEPH

Sarah shares a story about the time Joseph approached her about his "concerns over her weight." Sarah has always worked out. She has always had a regular workout routine and is always active. She was always smart about her dietary habits and always had the attitude that health was the most important element of fitness. If she were eating right and staying active, there was nothing to worry about.

Joseph was the exact opposite. He was a binger. He'd get on a health kick and then take it to the extreme – workouts, vitamin popping, no junk food; you get the idea. But, he'd always come off of the health kick and spend some time on the opposite extreme.

When it came to Sarah, Joseph liked to point out her flaws. He'd jump at the chance to call attention to a blemish, no matter how large or small. He had a habit of telling Sarah her clothes weren't sexy enough or that she looked frumpy. Any time she'd indulge or treat herself to a little food pleasure, he'd mention how it wasn't going to make her any thinner. One day he sat her down to discuss his growing concern over her weight.

"I'm just very concerned about your health. You look terrible. You haven't been exercising and all the weight you've gained makes you look fat. I'm just not attracted to you when your body looks like this. You really need to get back on an exercise plan."

"You think I look fat and I'm not exercising?"

"Well, just look at yourself. You can't afford to not be working out."

"I am working out. REGULARLY."

"I never see you working out."

"Maybe because I work out when you're not around."

Sarah laughed at him and showed him her workout log. Then she showed him how much she weighed on the scale, 130 pounds. Then she showed him her body mass index and the charts that show the range representing what a healthy body was for a woman of her height. Then she told him that HE had an unrealistic view of what a healthy woman looked like, that the anorexic/bulimic bodies that he identified as good looking were a reflection of HIS health, NOT HERS.

BEA'S FIREMOUTH

Bea was a young woman who had been with a *FIREMOUTH* for quite some time. Her friends begged and pleaded for her to throw him back, but under the influence of the abuse and in love with the idea of Tom and not the reality of Tom, Bea was trying to get pregnant. She INSANELY thought pregnancy would be a good idea; she reasoned that it would bring them closer, that he'd have to act differently as a father, and that their problems would magically resolve themselves. Getting pregnant to a *FIREMOUTH* is a TERRIBLE idea. Rather than one person to abuse, the abuser now has two to abuse, and now, also has more stressors and more bad-behavior triggers that might only result in MORE abuse. If you already have children with a *FIREMOUTH*—protect them and get out! It is your <u>obligation</u> as their guardian.

Abuse comes in many forms, including emotional, psychological, physical and sexual. If you are with a FIREMOUTH and are experiencing any of this do what you can to break away safely:

- ☐ You tip-toe around this person so you don't make him/her angry.
- ☐ Their buttons are pressed, and they're agitated for no apparent reason.
- ☐ They have a tantrum when they don't get their way.
- ☐ They're moody and/or have a temper.
- ☐ They try to make others feel bad for them.
- ☐ They suck the joy out of happy moments.
- ☐ They can't even answer normal questions without getting annoyed, irritated, or angry.
- ☐ They give back-handed compliments if they complement at all.
- ☐ They criticize more than compliment.
- ☐ They are angered when you don't agree with them.
- ☐ They won't take no for an answer.
- ☐ They bully you until they get their way.
- ☐ They try to talk for you.
- ☐ They expect to control all the plans.
- ☐ They tell you that you are the problem.
- ☐ They don't take responsibility for their actions.
- ☐ They blame others for their mistakes.
- ☐ They claim that people have always been out to get them, and just use and abuse them.
- ☐ Nothing is ever their fault.
- ☐ They are very critical of others.

☐ They demean others to build their self-esteem.

☐ They try to get you to help keep their dirty secrets for them.

☐ They keep secrets from you.

☐ They lie to keep control.

☐ They isolate you blatantly or sneakily.

☐ They try to diminish your confidence.

☐ They are jealous.

☐ They are physically abusive or threaten it.

☐ For more information on *FIREMOUTH*s, consult the following links:

☐ **National Domestic Violence Hotline**:

http://www.ndvh.org/
1.800.799.SAFE (7233) 1.800.787.3224 (TTY)
ANONYMOUS & CONFIDENTIAL HELP 24/7

☐ **Domestic Abuse Helpline for Men & Women**:

http://dahmw.org/

☐ **1-888-7HELPLINE (1-888-743-5754)**

☐ **Rape, Abuse & Incest National Network**:

http://www.rainn.org/ 1.800.656.HOPE

THE PENIS FISH

THE GUY WITH STDS

THE *PENIS FISH* IS THE COMMON NAME for a parasitic fish that lives in the Amazon. These fish are translucent and are difficult to detect, but they can certainly detect you! They detect chemicals the body lets off and then inject themselves into the target. Once they lodge themselves into the body cavity of the prey, they will make their way toward a blood source before exiting the body (if exiting is possible).

People who have been struck by a *PENIS FISH* didn't know it was coming because the translucent little creature is difficult to detect and it strikes before its victims ever see it coming. So, be in the know. When it comes to the man equivalent, that Penis could be carrying a number of invisible predators that are detrimental to your health!

Unfortunately you can contract a Sexually Transmitted Disease, STD, through oral, vaginal or anal sex (because the germs causing STDs, can live in saliva, blood, semen, and vaginal secretions). And some you can get merely by skin contact, such as genital warts and genital herpes. Contraction via skin contact is critical to understand because these diseases can be transmitted even when having protected sex. That is, if the bacteria or parasite is living on areas of the skin that come into contact during a sexual act, the disease can be spread. Let's face it—a condom doesn't cover everything!

If you're having any kind of sex with more than one partner, if that partner has had multiple partners, if you're not using condoms, and are careless when having sex you are putting yourself at high risk for an STD. It is important to know that some STDs, such as Trich—a parasitic disease, have an incubation period and therefore might not be detected right away. Some STDs are bacterial, (syphilis, gonorrhea, chlamydia) while others are viral (HIV, herpes, HPV, Hepatitis B). Of course, HIV is incurable, and while others are treatable, they can lead to serious problems if left undetected and untreated. Be SURE to schedule regular appointments with your doctor and screen for STDs if you're sexually active, and even if you've used protection. Do we really have to state the obvious? The only sure-fire way to prevent the spread of disease is by practicing abstinence. The higher the number of sexual partners—the greater the risk.

We're not telling you never to have sex. Sex is a great and an enjoyable activity between two consenting adults and it is your choice to partake or abstain. What we are telling you is to be in the know. Knowledge is power and it can help guide you at a time of great temptation—and keep you protected!

Don't think you can't feel pleasure if you practice abstinence. Don't think someone else has to be the source of your sexual pleasure. Ladies, a vibrator can be your BFF!

If taking control requires a trip (or two) to the local adult toy store to buy yourself a vibrator or other self-pleasure enhancing toys, don't be shy! Put your orgasms in your own hands! After all, vibrators don't kiss and tell…and as long as you keep a fresh supply of batteries they'll keep going… and going…

KNOW your Current Condition about your Sexual Health

☐ Speak openly to your partner about sex.

☐ Get tested and know your standing.

☐ Schedule regular check ups with your doctor.

☐ Protect yourself!

☐ Remember, oral, vaginal and anal sex ARE SEX!

☐ You have a CHOICE to abstain or to have sex.

☐ Masturbation IS a pleasurable and satisfying alternative!

Remember: After possible infection for HIV the body will begin to produce antibodies within 3-6 months. The production of those antibodies is how an HIV test determines whether you're negative or positive. *Therefore, in order to be sure that you and your partner are HIV free indeed, you need a period of abstinence (from all forms of sex and sexual activity) of 3-6 months.*

BLOWFISH

The Woman Who Lacks Self-respect & Integrity

Listen up ladies! You are not off the hook either! This one is aimed at all of us and is a reminder that we need to believe in our virtues and our self-worth and not tolerate inappropriate behavior no matter who the source, from men OR women.

School of Blowfish

The evening began pleasantly enough. It was hot and muggy, but the bar was crisp and cool. It was a building that had recently been remodeled and catered to a crowd of various ages, but mostly professionals and young adults. The conversation was smart, the atmosphere was mellow, and the drinks were not watered down. The evening had started off drama free. It's funny how quickly this can change. It's an interesting thing to observe a roomful of intoxicated people, whose inhibitions have been dulled by a few drinks. As we were observing the crowd, we noticed a Rainbow Fish, a Shark, a Pilot Fish… and an entire school of *BLOWFISH*.

There was a small group of women surrounding one guy. They seemed to be enjoying themselves based on their smiles, laughter and body language. The guy was clearly enjoying being the center of attention and was doing his best to keep them captivated. But then, he suddenly grabbed the head of the woman closest to him and began to bob her head up and down, just inches from his crotch, as he began a series of pelvic thrusts, simulating a public blow job. Classy move.

I was disgusted, not only over what he did, but also by the reaction of the group. Not one woman seemed to find the behavior offensive! Not one woman backed away, reprimanded, or responded with anything, but laughter and continued flirtation! I mean, what in the world would make such disrespectful behavior towards a woman acceptable?!

Talk about a need for raising the bar. C'mon ladies! We've got to hold men to higher standards than that! We've got to stick up for our sisters and make it clear that it is NOT acceptable or funny to degrade women on ANY level. We are NOT *BLOWFISH*!! I'll say it again—WE ARE NOT *BLOWFISH* and better behavior from men starts with what we tolerate and won't tolerate, what we accept and won't accept. Yes, he was the one who initiated such sexist behavior, but every woman there accepted it, and allowed themselves to be treated as objects.

MELON-CALLIE

Here's another example. I was walking on campus at a large State University a few years back and had the misfortune of listening to a young woman's conversation with her girlfriend. She was bragging that she had hooked up with some guy over the weekend and was ecstatic that this guy was all drooly over her. Hmmm, maybe it was the mass quantity of beer he had consumed and couldn't help but drool? –Just a thought!

Anyway, she was rambling on and ON about this guy! Now, I understand the excitement of meeting new people, and I understand why she liked the attention. What I didn't understand was why her self-esteem was so low and dependent upon this guy liking her because she had big boobs. YEP! Part of her rambling conversation was about how this guy had his eyes on her all night and wanted her so badly because she had huge ta-tas. *She found this flattering*. IMAGINE if we walked around telling men we had our eyes on them because they were sporting some wicked package!! C'mon ladies! A man pursuing you because you have big boobs is FAR from flattering! And women finding this behavior to be adequate, are pathetic and are *BLOWFISH!*

MARCELLO

One night while out with a friend of mine, I met a very attractive guy named, Johnson. He asked me for my number and, after chatting throughout the week I ended up going out with him. After spending the first part of the night out separately, we later met up with a couple of his friends, which led to my introduction to Marcello. Marcello was a very intelligent, courteous, and mild-mannered type of guy. As I chatted with him intermittently throughout the night, he projected this calm, peaceful type of energy. I don't think you could meet Marcello and not think, "*This is one hell of a nice guy.*" Even Johnson kept singing Marcello's praises by telling me he was the nicest guy he has ever met in his life.

Keeping this in mind, I watched Marcello as he decided to approach a group of girls and strike up a conversation. He must have spent approximately a half hour or so talking to several girls in the group. When he came back to us to give the lowdown on what had transpired, Marcello reported that several girls were actually very rude to him. They put him down and publicly embarrassed him.

Are you kidding me ladies?! These are the same girls that will whine and cry about how there are no nice guys out there or how horribly this guy or that guy treated her. Then she/they can turn right around and be mean for absolutely no reason, to a very nice guy that is standing right in front of them. Unbelievable! And you wonder why you only get jerks that treat you like crap! You choose them!

Now listen, I'm not saying a girl has to force herself to be with a guy that she clearly isn't interested in or attracted to. But would it kill 'ya to be kind? There's a difference between leading a guy on and just simply being nice because you yourself are a nice person. I mean is there *any reason,* what-so-ever to actually be mean to, embarrass, or demean a guy who simply tried to have a conversation with you? This is the type of guy girls "ruin." This guy has to wonder why he continues to be nice and *not* end up with a nice girl himself, when the *THROW BACK*s out there are the ones who end up with the girls. So, the "nice guy" eventually turns into a dick, I mean, a *THROW BACK* and treats girls almost as poorly as other *THROW BACK*s do because that's what girls seem to be attracted to.

This is so ass-backwards, I feel like I'm in the twilight zone when it comes to this stuff! Ladies, I have to give it to you straight: You are a human who has free will. You have the power to choose to be with a guy or not to be. If you, by your own free will, make the choice to be with a *THROW BACK,* then you better be woman enough to deal with it when he shits all over you. In my opinion you have forfeited the right to whine and cry and play victim. No, I don't feel sorry for the woman who chooses an obvious *PENIS FISH* over a hard-to-find nice guy, or **Big Tuna**. I also don't feel sorry for the "*BLOWFISH* in training," who cries one minute over how a guy treated her so poorly, and then turns around and is demeaning and disrespectful to a nice guy just because she isn't attracted to him.

We women need to learn to choose better, (or throw back the bad fish!), instead of saying "poor me" and making the same damn mistake all over again as soon as another *THROW BACK* gives us some attention. Put your efforts into finding those "good fish" and not releasing them once you've got 'em!! We can't raise the bar on good men if we don't even have a bar to raise!

Blow Your Fish or BlowFish-Itis

Another characteristic of a *BLOWFISH* is they flirt with taken men. Some do it in the presence OR absence of the guy's girl, with complete disregard for the relationship. Ladies, DO NOT FIGHT OVER A **catch**. If he's taken, he's taken and you have NO RIGHT to interfere. Have some self-respect and exercise some self-restraint… and then show some RESPECT for your sisters. Hitting on someone else's **catch** is despicable, disgusting behavior that shows a TRUE LACK OF CHARACTER ON YOUR PART. If this is how you behave then quite frankly, you deserve all the *THROW BACKS* that come your way.

I was out at a nightclub, dancing and enjoying a few drinks. My date and I were dancing together when this young woman began making eye contact with my guy. When there was enough room between us, she literally jumped in and threw her arms around my date. Granted, she did this with a number of different guys that evening, so she wasn't just focused on my date specifically, but the result was the same. She was sending the message that she didn't care what your situation was— if you wanted to score she was ready, willing and available. I remember feeling exasperated by her behavior and then sorry for her utter lack of self-esteem. Perhaps this book will reach women like her and impact them for the better.

Pro-ballers' wives make the same complaints about fans and the way they "approach" their men. Ladies, GET A HOLD OF YOURSELVES!! This behavior is UNACCEPTABLE and MUST STOP! We advocate "signing off."

To "sign off" is to acknowledge and accept a **catch** is taken, that a guy has something going on with someone, or to accept that one of your sisters is somehow already involved with a particular guy. It is a contract you will not interfere with what is already in motion. You vow not to interfere, to respect the situation, and to look elsewhere.

BLOWFISH:

- ☐ Hit on someone else's **catch.**
- ☐ Don't respect boundaries (their own OR other's).
- ☐ Tolerate and/or engage in disrespectful behavior by men.
- ☐ Have low self-esteem and are easily influenced by *THROW BACKs*.
- ☐ Sometimes dress like prostitutes and call it sexy.
- ☐ Are rude to and/or demeaning to nice guys.
- ☐ Are catty and see other women as competition.
- ☐ Are typically jealous, insecure women, who think they "gained" something by taking or trying to take someone else's man.
- ☐ Lack character, depth, sense of self, and integrity.
- ☐ Don't understand that TAKEN = TAKEN.
- ☐ Will fight over a **catch.**

ANGLERFISH

The Guy Who Lives a Double Life

Ivy & Isaac

Ivy was new in town. She had taken the leap and moved to a place she had always hoped to, a place where sunshine and warmth were abundant. She secured a new job where her talents would keep her climbing the ladder of success. She was respected, happy, and optimistic. She was exactly where she needed to be and wanted to be.

She got settled and then started exploring her new city. She left no stone unturned; restaurants, shops, local hot spots, every nook and cranny. She was loving life. She was a regular at the gym and was enjoying her dedication to her health and fitness as well. Everything was perfect! Until... *hello Isaac!* It looked like things were about to get even better,

Isaac was a long-term member at the gym Ivy joined. He was built... *very built*, was charming, and was also doing very well for himself selling real estate. He noticed the beautiful Ivy and started chatting her up. Chats lead to dates, which lead to a relationship, which lead to a proposal! Ivy was thrilled to have taken the risk to live her dream! She had everything she ever wanted! She was living a life beyond what she had hoped for, but her bubble was about to burst.

As they started getting closer, and their lives began to become more intertwined, Ivy began to notice little things that seemed "off." At first she couldn't explain it, and chalked it up to the jitters of things happening so quickly. However, there was always something nagging at her, and then another, and then another. They began to add up to the point she could no longer ignore them. She had to question what was really going on and knew she had to listen to her instincts.

Isaac claimed his wealth was due to his sharp skills in real estate. However, if that were the case, why did Ivy never see promotional signs anywhere? Why did she never see his name alongside a "for sale" sign? Why had she never been to his office? He never claimed to be an investor; he claimed to be an agent... so, what was up with all of that? And, why would a real estate AGENT have conferences all around the United States? Wouldn't the agent specialize locally? Wouldn't they need to know LOCAL markets and local laws to close property transactions? And don't agents have to have STATE licenses?

"So, tell me more about work. How are things going?" Ivy asked.

"Things are great! I am about to be recognized as top agent for most consecutive monthly sales," he boasted.

"That's great, babe! I look forward to meeting your colleagues. Are they having an award ceremony or luncheon, or something similar?"

"Yeah, at the conference next month, but it's out of town."

"You have another conference? You were just at a conference..."

Ivy knew there was something off about his story. In the meantime, other things seemed to be off as well. Isaac was getting text messages in the middle of the night that he claimed to be work-related. When questioned about this he was enraged, telling Ivy she had no right to interfere with his work. *"I do deals all over and have to be available whenever clients need me, any time, day or night."* When Ivy protested that a person still had to keep normal business hours and draw proper boundaries that allowed him to be off the clock, he claimed she was intrusive and meddling.

"This is disrespectful to me and the fact that we are in a relationship. Surely your clients will understand that text messages at 2am are NOT appropriate, REGARDLESS of the time change, but they are free to contact you during REGULAR business hours."

Isaac went ballistic and took off, and was 'incommunicado' for a couple of days.

When he got back he acted like nothing happened. He told her he was entitled to a cooling off period and that time away was good for the both of them. Needless to say, Ivy was getting depressed. None of this was acceptable behavior, and his outbursts and disappearances were becoming a habit, but they had a luxury home together in a gated community, very, very expensive cars, and were engaged to be married! Was she going to let all that go over what could just be growing pains? To make matters worse, she just found out she was pregnant.

The signs kept coming and the uneasiness kept growing with intensity. He would shut the computer when she'd come in the room and hide his phone. He had conferences that took him out of town ALL THE TIME. The more their lives intertwined, the more controlling he became. She wasn't allowed to maintain certain friendships from her past, yet he placed no such restrictions on himself. They had to be in the gym twice a day, without exception. She was discouraged from wearing makeup, certain hairstyles, or certain fashion trends, but... you guessed it... no such "dress code" applied to Isaac. The more she protested, the more she fought, the more Isaac cracked down. The more questions she asked, the more inconsistencies she found in his explanations.

So, Ivy went back to her roots. She went back to who she is and was BEFORE Isaac and returned to her true self. Ivy was a strong woman who had gotten side tracked as this THROWBACK seeped into her life. She focused on her gut feelings, and when she had a terrible feeling she'd act on it. She'd investigate it further in search of the truth and the truth was… she had an ANGLERFISH!

Those text messages? When the real estate you're selling is your body, then yes, they were about real estate.

Shutting down the computer? He had to hide the deals he was working with his sugar mamas AND his sugar daddies.

Conferences? More like rendezvous for the "sugar bucks" and meetings to appease the many clients he was entertaining!

This ANGLERFISH worked every angle, clients gave him money for fabricated sob stories like:

"His sick mother, whose medical bills were drowning the family in debt."

"The special needs dog he rescued from euthanasia."

"Paying tuition for the courses he was taking."

"Paying his bills."

"Flights to visit family he hadn't seen in years because in the minimum-wage job he worked he couldn't make ends meet."

Think of the most outrageous story you can come up with, and you've likely barely covered the angles this ANGLERFISH worked. He had hundreds of clients, and worked tirelessly to keep them all happy. Of course he did! When he's raking in around a half a million dollars a year, which he's not claiming at tax time, there's a lot at stake here!

When Ivy discovered the correspondences, she was in complete shock and disbelief. She could not believe she had reeled in an ANGLERFISH and really needed time to process her situation. She began to scour the web for anything she could find. At first she couldn't find anything on him outside of his personal accounts, but when she did, it became clear that the reason posting pics of their life on social networks had been strictly prohibited because it would blow his cover with his sugar-clients.

As she was researching she discovered that the dates of their arguments and subsequent disappearances corresponded with his rendezvous, the "conferences" were the same, and the out of state "real estate deals", were also sugar mamas and sugar daddies.

As if the fact that her fiancé had a double life, where none of his income was legit, wasn't enough to bear, Ivy had to deal with the health risks that this ANGLERFISH was subjecting her to through sexual relationships with multiple women AND men! Adding insult to injury, due to the steroids Isaac was injecting to maintain the body that would attract the paying clients, Ivy suffered a miscarriage that left her sterile.

Not even the award was real; he ordered it and paid for it as part of the façade that was (and continues to be) his existence.

Ivy's story has a happy ending. She threw back the nasty ANGLERFISH, allowing herself to live a life FREE of such toxicity. She is healing and returning to her true self, and is proud she had it in her to be strong enough to listen to her instincts and throw that pond scum back.

You might have an ANGLERFISH if:

☐ The bills are magically getting paid.

☐ There is a habit of disappearing for a few days without real explanation (or proof of story).

☐ The person is living by certain rules that don't seem to make sense (they're usually imposed upon them by the sugar mamas or daddies as requirement for sugar-bucks).

☐ They are secretive about not only their whereabouts, but also about whom they were with.

☐ They are sporting things they cannot afford on their own.

☐ They're taking vacations, eating at restaurants, buying clothes at places beyond their budgets.

☐ They're amassing massive amounts of wealth with no way to account for it.

☐ They won't allow you to meet their co-workers, colleagues, or friends tied to their "profession."

Be careful! ANGLERFISH have to be very, very meticulous in covering their tracks. They have to be sure that there is a certain amount of legitimacy in the lies they fabricate. Isaac went as far as to secure a real-estate license, but he also went out and bought props that would support his stories whenever he needed them. Peeling back the layers of lies the ANGLERFISH tale is difficult because they have to keep their transactions under wraps. By any other name this is prostitution, but they disguise it as a transaction that is just meant to "help a friend," or they create a scenario where they mimic a "relationship" so their bad behavior will stand up to the scrutiny of the law. They're creating loopholes so they can claim that what they're doing is legit. Bear in mind, however, there is always a power differential between the people involved. And this power differential leaves emotional and psychological wounds, and leaves an imprint of guilt and shame. How can it not when a person is allowing the ego to rule and dominate life? How can it not when the ANGLERFISH trades self-respect for degradation? Freedom for domination? Intimacy and love for exploitation? Self-worth for money?

SUCKER FISH

THE FOOL

THERE'S ANOTHER PROFILE that merits the spotlight, and that's the *SUCKER FISH*. The Sucker Fish is a person who has reeled in a *THROW BACK,* basically knows it, but makes every excuse in the book to justify the *THROW BACK'S* behaviors. The *SUCKER FISH* is so fixed on what they reeled in that they refuse to cut it loose. They ignore the never-ending stream of drama, negativity, stress, and dysfunction in favor of not being alone. They disregard lack of emotional support because they rationalize that they can seek that from their family or friends. The emotional, psychological, physical, or physiological discomfort that they experience as a result of time with their *THROW BACK* is something they work hard to ignore, gloss over, or attribute to other causes. They might allow name calling because the *THROW BACK* was "just having a bad day" or ghosting "because they just needed to cool off or have been super busy, so it really didn't count as disappearing". They accept that any little thing can throw the significant other into a tantrum or rage and shrug their shoulders because "it's just how they are" or because "they've been under a lot of stress or pressure lately." Or, when a *THROW BACK* doesn't accept responsibility for their actions, and then takes their frustrations out on their partner, says or texts hurtful things, and/or makes unreasonable demands the *SUCKER FISH* is such a sucker that no amount of these shenanigans is sufficient to call off the "relationship." Time after time they accept the behavior and might even jump through hoops to create a narrative that makes it palatable, and therefore ok to keep on keepin' on.

Abby & Aiden

This "relationship" started off on a foundation of dishonesty. Aiden was hiding an addiction. But he had met this beautiful, talented, smart woman, Abby, and he didn't want her to see what he was hiding. Furthermore, this woman turned out to be very willing to make excuses for him. She enabled him. Abby had immediately plunged into this relationship and since she was a busy woman herself she didn't notice the warning signs at first. Whenever Aiden would ghost her, he lied and told her it was because he was working. It turned out he was in no condition to meet up with her because he was nursing his addiction. When what he was hiding became evident, and that he had been lying from the start, rather than cut the line, she took him in and supported him. Her narrative was that he was "taking responsibility" and it would help him to become a "better person," that they would "grow as a couple" because relationships are full of ups and downs. She ignored the fact that Aiden was so selfish and self-absorbed that every interaction he had had with her was self-serving. She ignored that he showed complete disregard for the impact his choices had had on her and her life. She allowed the codependency to develop because there was no behavior she wouldn't tolerate from this *THROW BACK·* Her excuses for his poor choices and his treatment of her enabled him to continue to be that way.

ZACKARY & ZELDA

"But he needs me". That's how this messy entanglement played out because poor self-esteem is fodder for emotional manipulation. Zelda had pretty much everything going for her. She was financially independent, a professional, intelligent, and attractive; the whole nine yards. She randomly met Zackary while out one day, and even though he sent off a ton of intuitive alarm bells, she ignored them. The relationship was awkward from the start, but she brushed off the strange behavior. He was flamboyant at times to the point where it made others somewhat uncomfortable, and could be pretentious when he was in a mood, but his charm at other times somehow allowed the behavior to be swept under the rug. Over time, however, these small infractions of unacceptable behavior were painting an ominous picture, and more serious levels of emotional, psychological, physical abuse, and addiction were at play. But it was a picture that Zelda had been learning to justify along the way. Zelda's friends, however, weren't buying it. They were waving the red flags warning Zel of her poor choices, to the point that they began to distance themselves from her. But Zelda was too hooked. The cycle of breaking up, getting back together, the honey moon phase, and then the next series of arguments, and unbalanced, toxic, behavior would commence. Each time causing more and more damage to her self-esteem, and reinforcing the toxic, co-dependent, abusive dynamic between them. During one of the cycles Zackary revealed that he had a progressive illness, which only sent Zelda running back to him, since only "she knew how to care for him and he needed her" and she couldn't bear to leave him in such a condition on his own. The next inevitable break up happened but this time Zackary found a new woman to prey on. Zelda was distraught, trying to move on, but was really just waiting for the cycle to complete itself. She forfeited a healthy relationship and a chance with a true catch because she was still caught up in the toxic cycle that she just wasn't ready to let go of with Zachary. This was one *SUCKER FISH* who refused to cut the line.

JANE AND JONAS

Jane and Jonas are toxic in every sense of the term, and Jane is a textbook *SUCKER FISH.*

Jonas is a ghosting master. They get into an argument over pretty much anything since Jonas has lived his life with pretty much zero accountability. So when Jane alludes that Jonas should act like an adult, or if she questions his actions, Jonas just disappears. But that's ok with Jane! No matter how long he ghosts her, she takes him back. And, she takes him back after a stream of name calling arguments, nasty texts, being blocked on his phone from all forms of communication, you know, until he feels like talking again. And you can forget about Jonas taking responsibility for his actions (ghosting or the actions that sparked the original argument) – oh no- that will just lead to another round of the silent treatment! Oh, and never mind if Jane needs anything, like a friend to talk to, help, emotional support, the money he owes her. Those requests are enough to send Jonas through the roof. He doesn't have time for such things. But if he's had a bad day, Jane had better be there when he calls or needs to vent. I mean, if he needs comfort she'd better be prepared to ante-up and provide him with as much comfort and support as he was looking for. And it doesn't matter to Jane that they don't do anything as a couple! Oh no! Jonas always fails to show, cancels, changes the plans, and always has a reason why he can't be there or follow through. And this is perfectly acceptable to Jane! Oh yes… because she "loves him". However, when asked what she loves about an emotionally unavailable, emotionally immature, self-absorbed, individual who lacks empathy, personal insight and self-reflection, communication skills, and reliability… she doesn't want to answer. She says that she wants to find happiness, be married and have someone speak lovingly about her and act lovingly towards her, but she refuses to cut the line and throw Jonas back. This *SUCKER FISH* is ensuring she blocks herself from being a catch or finding a catch because she justifies toxicity rather than demanding healthy boundaries and balance, and allowing true loving behaviors into her life.

SUCKER FISH:

YOU are a *SUCKER FISH* if you have a *THROW BACK* and:

☐ Won't admit that you really don't feel so positive, supported, happy, safe etc. around your *THROW BACK·*

☐ Don't like to acknowledge that you experience emotional, psychological, and other types of distress with your significant other.

☐ Are drained by what you go through with your *THROW BACK·*

☐ Accept unnecessary challenges that your *THROW BACK* causes in your life.

☐ Go through constant break ups, followed by getting back together, and are ok with repeating this cycle.

☐ Put up with name-calling and can be quite crafty at finding ways to make being called horrible names ok.

☐ Ignore the fact that your *THROW BACK'S* actions do NOT match the whispering of sweet nothings into your ear.

☐ Don't hold your *THROW BACK* accountable.

☐ Make excuses for ghosting.

☐ Settle for being with a loser *THROW BACK* rather than being alone.

☐ Lack the self-confidence and self-esteem to set healthy boundaries

☐ Keep trying to convince yourself that you're strong enough to endure anything.

IN-BETWEENERS

THE GUPPY

THE EMOTIONALLY IMMATURE GUY

THESE GUYS DON'T HAVE harmful agendas and don't necessarily set out to take advantage of women but the end result of interacting with a *GUPPY* is still off-putting. They haven't taken the time to self-reflect, they don't know how they come across to other people and can be difficult to reach without bruising an already fragile ego. On the other hand, a *GUPPY* that takes the time to tackle his insecurities, grows on the inside, builds his self-esteem, and addresses his purpose, could transform into a **CATCH**. Therefore, beware of where the *GUPPY* is at the time you reel him in! An immature *GUPPY* is a *THROW BACK*! The *GUPPIES* below were all *THROW BACKs!*

DANIEL

Daniel was a government employee who spent most of his days

getting paid to surf the internet and contribute to the blog discussions of his favorite television programs. I'm not being sarcastic here—that is how he described *his own* work and *his own* day-to-day on the job. His knowledge about the characters, producers, episodes and what not, was pretty spectacular. He filled me in on many a missed episode and really kept me up to date.

It wasn't bad for a first date, but it wasn't very intellectually stimulating. While a fan of the same shows, I was by no means an avid viewer. Instead, I tuned in whenever I had the chance. Although it wasn't an incredibly interesting first date, he had been nervous and was a gentleman so I agreed to meet up and see how round two would play out.

We met up again about a week or so later and this time Daniel put all his cards on the table. He told me he'd like me to be his girlfriend so we could start thinking about marriage and what we wanted long term. He was ready; he liked me, and thought we should get started. Clearly there was no time to lose... apparently like, getting to know one another!

Now remember our first date was spent talking about television shows and our second date was spent talking about weddings. I wasn't sure at what point I stepped out of reality and into the twilight zone, but I was there nonetheless. I didn't even know how to respond to the situation and tried my best to keep the focus on him. I figured if he kept talking then it would take the pressure off of me.

I headed home that night replaying the sequence of events in my head. It seemed even crazier in retrospect. It still doesn't even seem real as I retell it now, but it happened.

I didn't see Daniel after that, truthfully, I really couldn't bear it. He bombarded me with email and online messages, but I just couldn't respond. I didn't even know how to!

Solomon

Solomon created a big-fish-small-pond scenario for himself by ensuring he was surrounded by a younger, less educated crowd. Then he would use words that he guessed no one would understand and then belittle them when they were baffled. Not only did this small fry try to use "big" words, but he also went around correcting people's grammar. Whoa!! Go around correcting random people's grammar and you're sure to make friends fast. So you can only imagine how popular this guy was! Yep! The quintessential *cold fish!*

For example, a group of acquaintances gathered in a coffee shop one day. As they perused the pastries he turned to them and said, "*These pastries look rather mellifluous[1]. Do YOU think they look mellifluous?*" As they looked at him with that "who says that look," I interjected by placing my order.

On another occasion we were about to head out after having lunch when he said he needed a minute to grab his satchel. His SATCHEL?! Are you kidding me? I mean, how many people do you hear refer to their MAN PURSE as a satchel?!

I took a breath and counted to ten, but as I thought about all the people he has insulted with his "big" words, I couldn't help myself and I began to howl with laughter before the ten seconds were up!

"A satchel? A **satchel**?! <u>Why</u> are you using that word? Not only is it a grandpa word, but what you're carrying is NOT a satchel!!"

He didn't find the situation as amusing as I did. I think he didn't want me to *know* what a satchel was, or more accurately he didn't want me to know he was using his "big" word incorrectly!

Over time it became clear that Solomon made it a common practice to

---

1   Mellifluous = something containing honey that is smooth, and decadent.

one-up everyone he came in contact with. His use of uncommon words or phrases and his constant attempts to act superior over others was unnecessary. Sol was a likeable guy who was lacking more in wisdom than character. For Sol, a little self-reflection and a look at himself through the eyes of others would change his interpersonal circumstances in unforeseen ways.

DAN'S COLLEAGUE

I was walking through a busy, congested and crowded airport a few years back. I had disembarked and was making my way to my next flight. After trying to find a safe place to step onto the already over-crowded escalators, I wound up stepping right in front of a "gentleman," who began to yell to a buddy of his who was about five people in front of me.

"Did you see that plane of Hooter girls?" he yelled.

*"Hey, Dan. Dan! Did you **SEE** that plane of Hooter girls?!"*

Dan turns to look at his buddy who is now gesturing in a way that suggested the ladies were triple Z in size.

I threw a side-ways glance with a furrowed brow at the man behind me.

He smirked and let off a snicker.

"Dan! I mean, you should've seen the rack on these girls!"

I turned and faced the man directly, looking straight into his eyes.

"Ha! I guess some people are getting a little upset," he bellowed. All the ladies around me became visibly tense.

I turned to face him and asked, *"Sir, how big is your penis?"*

His eyes widened.

"Maybe you didn't hear me the first time. I asked *you, sir, how BIG is your penis? I mean, I'm standing here with a full view of your junk and I'm not seeing much package going on."*

His jaw dropped and he stammered.

"I hope it is much bigger erect." I sarcastically commented.

At this point the man is visibly embarrassed.

"Oh!" I said. *"When the tables are turned you're uncomfortable!* **You** *don't like being objectified, interesting coming from a man whose willing to shout about women's breast sizes in public. Maybe next time you'll think before you open your mouth."*

By then we had reached the end of the escalator. The women stepped off with a giggle. The man exited in silence, and I continued on knowing that I put a stop to bad behavior—at least for that moment.

RYAN

Ryan is a nice guy. He is looking for love and is disappointed by all the THROW BACKS he's encountering. He does have a good sense of self, is scrupulous, hard-working, and decent. His philosophy is that relationships are really about two people willing to commit and learn about how to grow together. He is so close to being a catch! But, his issue is that when he meets someone he likes, he's all about getting his needs met. Every text, every instance in which he initiates communication is with one objective – to get HIS needs met. The pleasantries that typically are exchanged as a way to connect and follow up on conversations are really initiated with the goal of getting what he wants. The interest is disingenuous; he's not sincerely interested in how X, Y, Z are going, what he really wants to know is when his date is going to be available. On the surface, his messages seem sweet and thoughtful, but they are always followed with making sure that time is taken away from X, Y, Z so that he gets some of his love interest's attention. What Ryan doesn't understand is that being pushy is a turn off. He also doesn't understand that it is easy to see his intentions. Trying to dictate how someone should spend their time isn't going to bring one of his love interests any closer to him. In fact, NOT giving them the space to pursue their passions drives them away each and every time. If he doesn't respect that a woman has her own interests, goals, and friends and knows how to structure her own time, he will remain in the Guppy classification. Being able to recognize and support another is critical for a healthy relationship, and understanding that if two people are going to grow together, the interaction has to consist of more than just one party trying to get their needs met without regard for things that matter to the other.

GUPPIES are difficult to categorize because there are so many varieties. Here are a few characteristics to watch out for:

- ☐ He subtly belittles others to boost his self-esteem.
- ☐ He fronts a superior attitude, yet people often view him as socially awkward.
- ☐ His ringtone for you is the *wedding march & he subscribes to Groom magazine.*
- ☐ He carries the wedding binder in his car.
- ☐ He is pre-registered at Bed Bath & Beyond.
- ☐ He thinks he knows what he wants before all the information is in.
- ☐ Has no idea of his place in the world … except to be in yours.
- ☐ Doesn't know that PC is an acronym for "politically correct."
- ☐ Is surprised when people find him annoying.
- ☐ Has tunnel vision when it comes to getting HIS needs met

MINNOWS

IMPRESSIONABLE YOUNGSTERS

I'LL NEVER FORGET my interactions with a first grade class in Philadelphia. As the students were standing in line to go to art class, I heard one six-year-old boy say to a little girl, "I'm a playa! I'm a playa! Back up trick. Make room for me." When I asked him where he learned to speak that way, he told me his older brother. When I asked him how old his brother was, he told me he was 10. Talk about impressionable.

MINNOWS gather information like a sponge. They observe interpersonal relationships in real life and through the media and need help deciphering their observations. Unfortunately, to some people it might seem our kids are too young to have discussions about sex and romantic relationships. But they are impressionable and age-appropriate discussions are important factors in their personal growth and future sexual health and outlook.

The young people who inspired these fish tales came from families who had spoken to their children about the birds and the bees to some capacity, but the conversations still didn't register with the kids. One night at dinner, Nina asked her son if he was sexually active or if he was experimenting sexually. He told his mother he wasn't sexually active. In his words he, "*only got a blow job and went down on a girl.*" Another mother asked her daughter if she were having sex, and the daughter said NO because she had only given a blow job and had had anal sex. After a conversation about this, the daughter reasoned it wasn't sex if she couldn't get pregnant! Many teens are sexting (sending sexually provocative text and video cell phone messages) without an understanding that their actions are considered in many states to be production and distribution of child pornography.

Luckily, there are guardians who do protect our youth. I heard a story of two teenagers who frequented a local Under-21 club, who got kicked out for inappropriate and lewd behavior. The two of them were exploring each other in the middle of the dance floor. The boy had his hands up the girl's skirt and under her panties. When the owner became aware of this he flipped on the lights, grabbed the teens, and cleared out the club. He sent a clear message that such behavior was NOT acceptable or tolerated in his club. He then called the kids' parents and had them picked up. Kudos!

Even worse is the current trend for teens to have sex with each other in the middle of the dance floor of their school dances, while others circle around them and watch. Outlandish and dangerous sexual behaviors are happening younger and younger.

Please don't overlook *MINNOWS!* Small fish are vulnerable to larger, more cunning hunters and need to be armed with age appropriate, factual information about the human body, sex, and interpersonal relationships (platonic and romantic), self-love, self-esteem, and other important matters. They need to know that sex is sex is sex, no matter the point of entry.

They need to know the kind of message twerking sends, and have the ability to distinguish between trashy behavior and classy behavior. They need exposure to people who are sexy because they are classy, smart, and poised so they don't come to the false conclusion that sexy means being, looking, and acting trashy. We have the responsibility to expose them to more than the raunchy, tasteless, garbage that is so readily available. We have the responsibility to present them with other models; models that boost their self-esteem. Models that ease insecurities, models that venerate tasteful behavior, while still being edgy and artistic. It is up to us! Let's step it up!

MINNOWS:

- ☐ Young and impressionable.
- ☐ Need your guidance and protection.
- ☐ Need supervision and open-door communication.
- ☐ Need age appropriate information about sex and interpersonal relationships.
- ☐ Are **catches** or *THROW BACK*s in-the-making.

FLOUNDER

"I WANT TO BE WITH YOU. I DON'T WANT TO BE WITH YOU. I WANT TO BE WITH YOU. I DON'T WANT TO BE WITH YOU. I WANT TO….."

IT'S BEEN SAID THAT MEN fear commitment because they see it as a loss of freedom. That is, while single the only pressures they have are the ones they place on themselves. Talk about a boys-will-be-boys upbringing that raises narcissists! Relationships are about BOTH parties having to make the effort to make things work. Some men say they worry about their individuality and identity, their time with friends, that you won't respect them, and then you'll turn out to be crazy, AND THEN you'll be the only woman he'll get to have sex with for the rest of his life!

Essentially, they fear growing up, and they fear intimacy!! And why *wouldn't* they???!!! In a society where we allow the boys-will-be-boys behaviors, where we lower standards and don't prepare boys to be accountable for their behavior, responsible to others, in tune with their emotions, etc. we ARE NOT ADEQUATELY PREPARING them for healthy, interpersonal relationships.

While they might love and adore you, the transition might be very difficult. A male friend of mine, Edwin, said women socialize men... that when a man finds someone he really loves he'll shape up and develop the emotional skills and personal attributes that will ensure a successful relationship.

"Women socialize men. Boys become men when they want the attention of a woman because unless they begin to act like a man she won't give him the time of day. Therefore, when he's really into you, he'll grow up!"

Why not? He stands to gain self-worth, self-confidence, self-esteem, purpose and intimacy when he rises to the task, and in turn, stands to GREATLY IMPROVE his quality of life. When men mature *they benefit* from committed relationships! A report from Cornell University stated:

"Being married is associated with higher self-esteem, greater life satisfaction, greater happiness and less distress, whereas people who are not in stable romantic relationships tend to report lower self-esteem, less life satisfaction, less happiness and more distress..."[2]

If he can develop his emotional awareness, the *FLOUNDER* can *flip* himself, and transform himself, into the ultimate **catch**, the **Big Tuna**. In opting for a mature, loving, committed relationship he'll gain the love, respect, and admiration he truly desires. If the couple accentuates the positive elements of each other and their experiences together, they have the key elements for a happy, joyful, successful, long-term relationship. However, if the *FLOUNDER* can't do what it takes, he'll retreat to feelings of inadequacy, vulnerability, and the like. As a result of these negative feelings he'll attempt to compensate through destructive behaviors, where he'll attempt to control, manipulate and dominate. That is, he'll *flop* into *THROW BACK* behavior and end up putting himself in a position where he cannot enjoy the single most important source of satisfaction, pleasure, happiness, contentment and fulfillment in life—an intimate, committed relationship.

---

2   http://www.news.cornell.edu/stories/Dec05/relationships.happy.ssl.html

The following stories are of *FLOUNDERS* who were able to, and willing to, take the plunge and have lived VERY HAPPILY because they did.

Kyle & Tamera

Kyle knew he was floundering. He and **Tamera** had known each other for years as friends, and had already been dating for quite a while by the time the beach weekend rolled around. Little did he know that his floundering was about to get him thrown back! Little did he know that if he couldn't quit behaving like a fish out of water —and cut the flip flopping—*by that weekend* he'd be back on the market, on ice, packed in like a sardine with all the other lonely bachelors. Tamera had reached her limit and was ready to cut him loose, but they had planned this beach weekend well before she realized she might have to cut the line. She decided they might as well have one final memorable weekend together before calling it quits. Besides, that would give him one last and final chance to QUIT floundering and take the relationship to the next level— marriage.

What Tamera didn't know was Kyle was starting to sense that his time was up. He knew Tamera was a no-nonsense woman who would not settle for anything less. He knew she was a **catch** and he was lucky to have her and he knew he could not continue to *FLOUNDER* forever, lest he wind up a sad and sorry man. So, in anticipation of the beach weekend he went out and bought an engagement ring and concocted a plan to propose to her when she'd least expect it.

Before heading south they each spoke to Tamera's parents. Tamera told her mother that since things weren't going anywhere she planned to end it while she still had the time, energy and interest in getting back to the dating scene. She told her mother she had waited long enough and if they were in different places that she could deal with that, but he wasn't going to take up any more of her valuable and precious time. Well, her mother knew Kyle was going to pop the question because he had spoken with her too! "Don't do it until **after** the weekend," she warned… explaining that it would be an unkind thing to do and it would tarnish their possibly, final time together.

Tamera agreed because it was reasonable and she did love him and didn't want to end things on a sour note. They could have their last weekend of fun and she could give him the final chance to come around.

Kyle knew he was going to pop the question, but he wanted it to be a surprise and he knew surprising Tamera would be extremely challenging! He sensed it was time and he was finally ready, which was lucky for him because he didn't know until a while later how close he came to being a *THROW BACK* instead of a **Big Tuna**!

Anyway, Friday night rolled around and Kyle had decided he'd propose on *Saturday*. Well, this caused great anxiety for Tamera because it seemed he didn't have a ring after all. And believe you me—SHE WAS LOOKING! She tried to get him to put their valuables in the hotel safe, but of course Kyle had nothing. She *double checked* that he had everything covered and in a safe place before they left the hotel to meet up with friends and she found nothing! Kyle had his work cut out for him. He was hiding the ring in crazy places and carrying it with him (carefully) so there was no way to find it because he *knew* Tamera was fishing for evidence of a ring!! His efforts paid off! When the rooting around didn't reveal anything, Tamera thought there was a big fat breakup in store for Monday! She became frustrated and the two began to bicker, only Kyle was trying to stay on her good side because he was looking for the right moment! Thank God for Saturday night because Kyle asked Tamera to be his wife *just in the nick of time!*

The rest of the weekend was spent in celebration. They had a blast at their wedding and have had fun ever since! They're a joy to be around and when they tell the story of the proposal they laugh at how it all played out! Kyle went from floundering to being a great **catch** and is now a proud husband and doting father of a beautiful baby girl.

UNCLE KASEY & AUNT JACEY

Our **Uncle Kacey** and **Aunt Jacey** met when they were teenagers. Aunt Jacey is almost four years older than Uncle Kasey, but the difference didn't matter. She was smitten and he was one lucky man! Our Uncle was <u>such</u> a player and was tremendously popular, not only because of his good looks, but also because of his sense of humor and his charisma. He's someone people really enjoy being around to this day! He is a man of integrity, but age does factor into the quality of the decisions we make, and as a young guy some of his decisions weren't so great.

For instance, the time he drank a bottle of whiskey our granddad had brought back from overseas. Granddad was saving that bottle, for no special occasion, because it was a memento he cherished. It reminded him of a certain time in his life and the experiences that were born out of it. However, all a teenaged uncle saw was easy access to booze and so he drank it up and filled the bottle with some other liquid to a level that would go undetected as long as the bottle were still in its box! Granddad was devastated when he discovered the bottle had been opened, but he was even more devastated when he discovered the good stuff had been replaced with a placebo!

Or the time he went out in a fluorescent green t-shirt with black felt letters that said PARTY NAKED.

Or when I caught him smoking cigarettes and blackmailed him to pay up to keep me quiet but he missed a "payment" thinking he didn't have to take blackmail from a five-year old seriously...*he was wrong!*

Or the blue shag carpeting he used to line the bed of his van.

Anyway, the point is at some point in all of this fun, Uncle Kasey and Aunt Jacey got together and wound up pregnant. Clearly the two were meant to be together, but at such a young age there were many obstacles to overcome. Aunt Jacey handled them like a true **Angel Fish**.

In the beginning Uncle Kasey was floundering and acting like a damn *THROW BACK*. He was not willing to let go of the fun and face the sobering reality before him. So, Aunt Jacey threw him back and went on with her life! But, she was VERY SMART about it.

Aunt Jacey was able to kill two birds with one stone. She was able to ensure that Uncle Kasey got quality time with his daughter, and she was able to let him know *she wasn't sitting around waiting for him.* When she had a date planned, Uncle Kasey had additional father-daughter time. It was *brilliant* because everyone benefitted AND he got to see just what he couldn't have as long as he was behaving like a *THROW BACK*! This lasted about a year before things turned around and Uncle Kasey showed signs of being a **Big Tuna**.

He started coming around more often, had even broken up with his girlfriend, and was not dating anyone else. Now, he didn't tell Aunt Jacey this right away, but rather, he asked her to spend Valentine's Day together!

"What about your girlfriend?" She asked.

"We broke up a while back," he informed.

She told him that for Valentine's Day she wanted to date each other exclusively.

"How about for Valentine's Day you don't date anyone but me, and I don't date anyone but you?" She suggested.

"Ok," he said.

And that was that! They were together officially. The next big step came when Aunt Jacey's birthday was coming up. When Uncle Kasey asked her what she wanted for her birthday she replied with, "An engagement ring." He replied with, "Ok." They were married in September of that year.

This story is a prime example of women socializing men. Until he behaved well enough to get her attention, Aunt J. kept Uncle K. at a distance. Once he began to act like a respectable man and show his good side, she slowly let him in. That friend of mine who told me that women socialize men, that when a man wants to be with a woman badly enough he will learn how to behave. He was spot on. In this story, it worked like a charm.

So, ladies, if you'd rather act like a *BLOWFISH* than an **Angel Fish**, you will only **catch** *THROW BACKS*, you will have a tough time finding your **Big Tuna** because you are sending off signals about how men can treat you, the kind of behavior you accept, and what you think about yourself! Aunt Jacey knew this instinctively and made all the guys who were crazy for her, BEHAVE to get her attention. She is a gorgeous woman who is smart and cheery. She could have had her pick easily and she had many a fish trying to get her attention. Even so, she was *very careful* to choose only the ones who <u>were not</u> on the *THROW BACK* list. It worked, because in the end she got her **Big Tuna**, and through it all she maintained her standards, her dignity and her self-respect.

LUCAS

Lina and her friend were out to lunch when they met Lucas. They happened to be at the same place at the same time, as luck would have it. Lina's friend pointed out that Lucas was flirting with her and encouraged her to take note. Lina didn't buy it, but Lucas was good looking and seemed to have the personality to back up his looks, so… she flirted back.

Lucas encouraged her to stop by the same place to listen to a band that was scheduled to play the following weekend. Lina couldn't make it, but decided that she'd stop in another time and see if their paths crossed. It took a while but, they did meet up again. Lucas decided to asker her out directly, and she accepted.

Lucas and Lina got to know each other over about two years. Right after they met Lucas was moving out of town to begin a degree program. It was a long-standing goal of his that he had been working hard to achieve. But the distance was welcomed. Lina had already graduated and having been in his shoes she was excited for him. Besides, it was a great opportunity to also learn about how deeply their intellectual, emotional, and potentially romantic connection could be.

And so, they kept in touch. When Lucas returned home to visit family, he and Lina spent quality time together. They certainly had a healthy and positive connection, with certain overlapping experiences that should have brought them closer. They had amazing sexual chemistry as well, with each having a solid value system, similar life philosophies, common interests, and content of character to back it all up!

But, Lucas was *FLOUNDERING*. Lina was a catch and Lucas had **Big Tuna** potential but he struggled to move closer to Lina. Somewhere on the road he was afflicted with the "there's plenty of fish in the sea" syndrome and failed to recognize the scale of the catch that was right there in front of him.

Sadly, such an affliction limits growth to a perpetual "seeing what happens" stage and after a while ensures that intimacy cannot take root. Sometimes *FLOUNDERS* miss out something that could be amazing simply because they fail to recognize what is right in front of them. Unfortunately, Lucas flopped into a *THROW BACK* rather than flipping into a **BIG TUNA.**

FLOUNDER:

- ☐ Flip – Floppers: The ones willing to grow up, can flip into being a **Big Tuna**, the ones who refuse to, flop into *THROW BACK* status.
- ☐ Potential **Big Tuna.**
- ☐ Potential *THROW BACK·*
- ☐ Love and adore their **catch,** but are having trouble moving forward with their **Angel Fish** to official status (and/or) marriage.

CATCHES: ANGEL FISH & BIG TUNA

ANGEL FISH

THE FEMALE PERFECT CATCH!

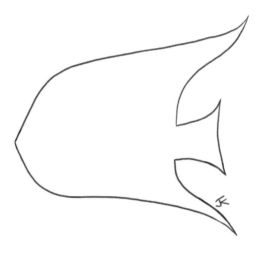

We're so close to getting to the **Big Tuna**! Before we do, let's remember ladies that the purpose of this book is, ultimately, EMPOWERMENT. It is to awaken your instincts, raise your standards and empower you not to settle for pond scum. Are we blaming you for outlandish, male, *THROW BACK* behavior? OF COURSE NOT! What we *are* doing is holding you responsible for *accepting* these behaviors; possibly feeding into these behaviors, and for NOT throwing back the men who act out these behaviors into the dark depths of the sea!

Let's be honest, you can't expect to be with a **Big Tuna,** nor do you necessarily deserve one, if you yourself are not an **Angel Fish**. Each and every one of us is unique and should be proud of what makes us stand out from other women. However, there are some fundamental principles that make up the foundation of what an **Angel Fish** is. This is what every woman should be able to identify with and what every girl should aspire to be. You're never too young to begin to learn the attributes of an **Angel Fish**, nor are you ever too old to change into one.

To all of those **Big Tunas** out there, your **Angel Fish** is a woman who:

- *Respects you and loves you for who you are.*
- *Has that sparkle in her eyes when you enter the room.*
- *Is your best friend as well as your lover.*
- *Has depth of character and a personality that complements yours.*
- *Has integrity.*
- *Has self-respect.*
- *Is kind, compassionate, open and honest; demonstrates transparency.*
- *Shows you appreciation for all that you do for her.*
- *Reminds you why she loves you and what she admires about you.*
- *Makes you feel good about the man that you are.*
- *Inspires you to continue to grow and be the best man you can possibly be.*
- *Knows herself.*
- *Trusts her instincts and listens to her intuition.*
- *Is independent and her own person.*

Remember! **Angel Fish** *respect themselves AND other women, they don't fight over the* **catch***, they understand TAKEN = TAKEN, and hold men to high standards of respectful behavior, filled with integrity.*

CHARACTERISTICS OF **ANGELFISH**: A Checklist

☐ Able

☐ Assertive

☐ Balanced

☐ Compassionate

☐ Communicative

☐ Confident

☐ Considerate

☐ Courteous

☐ Decent

☐ Fair

☐ Generous

☐ Honest

☐ Independent

☐ Intuitive

☐ Intolerant of Bad Behavior

☐ Kind

☐ Levelheaded

☐ Mature

☐ Modest

☐ Poised

☐ Polite

☐ Reasonable

☐ Realistic

☐ Reliable

☐ Respectable

☐ Responsible

☐ Scrupulous

☐ Sensible

☐ Sincere

☐ Self-assured

☐ Stable

☐ Strong

☐ Supportive

☐ Trusting

☐ Trustworthy

☐ Virtuous

☐ Vulnerable

☐ Wise

The BIG TUNA

THE ULTIMATE CATCH!

To all men out there, if you are behaving as a *THROW BACK* then you certainly don't deserve to be with an **Angel Fish**. If you are someone who really would like to be in a fulfilling relationship with someone you can "take home to the family," then you first need to evaluate yourself and your behaviors. You truly attract what YOU are. Be honest in identifying what kind of fish you are and what changes you need to make to become a **Big Tuna**. You may also need to assess what school you're swimming in and what types of fish you're swimming with. If you're swimming with a bunch of *DOG FISH* and *SLIPPERY DICKS*, then how do you expect to attract an **Angel Fish**? Not only that, but your chances of ever becoming a **Big Tuna** yourself are significantly hindered because, let's face it, your friends truly are a reflection of who YOU are.

Guys, when hanging out with a bunch of rotting fish, before you know it, you're so far out from shore that's it's hard to come back and become a **Big Tuna**. Because of this you may never find an **Angel Fish**. So, we're going to make it easy for you! Remember, there is no one-size-fits-all when it comes to the **Big Tuna**! The **Big Tuna** comes in countless varieties and is different for everyone, but all **Big Tunas** have some things in common.

Guys, this is what you should strive to be and girls, when deep-sea-fishing for your **Big Tuna**, this is what you should look for:

- He's the man who loves and respects you; he treats you with dignity, respect, and admiration.
- He's the man whose days are brighter because you're a part of it.
- He's open, honest, kind and considerate.
- He has depth of character.
- He compliments you and leaves you feeling good after you've spent time with him.
- He has similar philosophies on life, love, religion, politics, money, family, child rearing, and all the things important to the relationship you want to build.
- He realizes there are many reasons to be in a bad mood, not just because of PMS. After all, he realizes that he can be pissy too!
- Where there are differences he is willing to negotiate, compromise and put your needs selflessly ahead of his own.
- He communicates with you no matter how difficult it may be to express his feelings.
- He's loyal and trustworthy.
- He's not afraid/embarrassed to show affection or compliment you in front of others, (particularly his guy friends).
- He's man enough to be respectful of women when "with the guys" or when he's not in your presence.
- He treats you as an equal partner.
- He defends and protects you.

- He *always* puts you first, even in front of his mother!
- He is your ***friend and lover***, not just a lover.
- He doesn't selfishly think that sex is over just because HE had an orgasm. It's important to him to satisfy you sexually and emotionally.

CHARACTERISTICS OF **BIG TUNAS**: A Checklist

- ☐ Can Draw Proper Boundaries
- ☐ Communicative
- ☐ Compassionate
- ☐ Conducts Himself Appropriately
- ☐ Considerate
- ☐ Emotionally Engaged & Present
- ☐ Faithful
- ☐ Generous
- ☐ Giving
- ☐ Good Impulse Control
- ☐ Has a Working Moral Compass
- ☐ Honesty
- ☐ Integrity
- ☐ Intolerant of Slippery Dicks & Throw Back Behaviors
- ☐ Levelheaded
- ☐ Mature
- ☐ Reasonable And Rational
- ☐ Scrupulous
- ☐ Selfless
- ☐ Sincere
- ☐ Strength of Character
- ☐ Strength to Resist Peer Pressure
- ☐ Supportive and Reassuring
- ☐ Trustworthy
- ☐ Virtuous
- ☐ Well-Mannered, Courteous, Polite

A BIG TUNA STORY

PAUL K. YOHE, II

OUR GRANDFATHER HAS EARNED this title because the love he has and had for our grandmother touches our hearts deeply. They had always had a certain dynamic with one another, each one insisting on their own version of the story, with the two of them laughing to tears at how the other one viewed it! We loved the banter and used to anticipate it eagerly whenever they told their stories.

Our grandparents were married for over 50 years! They met as teenagers, raised four children, helped out with the grandchildren, and still stayed involved in their own activities.

No matter how great a relationship, and no matter how much love there is, there are always tough times. Our grandmother had weight-management issues that she never quite got under control. With as large as she got, and considering the numerous health problems she endured as a result, it was amazing how well her body endured!

The last few years of her life were filled with ups and downs. She had passed the point of no return physically, but her spirit was alive and well. At some point, she was almost completely confined to a lift-chair because her joints could no longer withstand the weight of her body. She had had numerous operations to restore her vision; which had been fading as a result of diabetes.

Grandma's health circumstances changed the way my grandparents had to care for one another. Their roles changed. Granddad became the cook and the caregiver, while grandma became the receiver in a way she had never experienced before. It was difficult for them. Age and aging was a stark reality they could not ignore.

In time, they adjusted to their new routines and their bond grew even stronger. The two established a schedule and granddad learned to revolve his daily activities around the needs of my grandmother—-when she needed to eat, take her insulin, take her meds, etc. But eventually, the day arrived; the day we all knew was the beginning of the end for our grandmother. She went into the hospital in late January and never came out. She died in March without a last chance to return to the life she had known for 72 years.

Granddad took it as well as he could, but it was clear he was experiencing a most devastating blow. The woman he adored and loved so deeply was cruelly removed from his life and this time she was not bouncing back.

We hugged our grandfather and told him we loved him, and that while physically gone, assured him grandma lived on in our memories and in our hearts, and would continue to live on for as long as we all remembered her and cherished her. He turned his teary gaze to meet ours and began to talk about *freedom*.

There is no freedom like the tie that binds you to another person. There is no freedom like the responsibility you have for someone else's well being, for someone else's heart. I remember feeling frustrated at times that I had to be here or there, or I had to do this or that, and couldn't just do what I wanted when I wanted. I thought that that was freedom. But the truth is, loving someone one is freedom. Loving someone through the good and the bad, loving someone deeply, loving someone to where you can put their needs above or on par with your own, THAT is FREEDOM. With her death, I've lost my freedom and if she could come back to me tomorrow I'd ask her to do it all over again.

We can't even retell that story without getting teary eyed and lumps in our throats because we are convinced he is right and we're convinced it's true! So, while we're on the path for our **Big Tuna** we can only hope to find the one that would make the **King Tuna**, Mr. Paul K. Yohe, II proud.

CLOSING REMARKS

1. LEARN TO LISTEN TO YOUR INSTINCTS

There is a big difference between listening to your fears, your worries, your friends or family telling you what you should do and your actual INSTINCTS. Instincts act as your true guidance system if only you'd pay attention to them. Isn't it amazing that you can look back on a failed relationship and realize that the signs were always there that he had been cheating? Yet you had ignored them because you didn't want to face what your instincts were telling you. Hindsight is only 20-20 because you chose to ignore your intuition during the time you needed to open your ears and your heart to hear it.

Remember, when we ignore our instincts about "Mr. Wrong," simply because we *want* him to be "Mr. Right," the end result will be a less fulfilling relationship or even a failed one.

When a guy who is really attractive, masculine, and wanted by many other women, pays attention to you, it can be exhilarating. You get butterflies in your stomach. It's elating because you feel like you may have found a good **catch**, a potential **Big Tuna**. It can also make you feel special that you caught the attention of a Big Fish in the pond you swim in.

However when the signs are there that this guy, although sexy, popular, and wanted by half the girls you know, may not actually be a good **catch**, something seems to happen to "today's women" encouraging her to ignore all of those signs and refrain from acting on them.

When you get an uneasy feeling about something, your instincts are speaking to you. When something seems "just not quite right," but you can't explain why; those are your instinctual warning signals that need to be paid attention to and taken seriously. The worst thing you can do is ignore them and continue on like everything is okay. Don't turn into foolish girls and throw your blinders on. Refrain from over-analyzing the situation to death. Don't discuss for hours on end with your friends about what you should do because you already know you should throw him back. Your intuition is the best source of advice. Listen to it and stop worrying about trying to make sense of it or explaining it to other people. Sometimes a "*THROW BACK* decision" doesn't really make sense at the time, but you chose to listen to your instincts anyway. More often than not you'll eventually come to find your sixth-sense was right and the guy turned out to be a *THROW BACK*.

Everyone has intuition. Everyone. This is your own, personal guidance system. But, few hone-in and sharpen their intuitive skills. Most have done the opposite; ignored their natural intuition to the point where they can't even hear it most of the time and possibly can't even hear it at all. It's time to relearn how to discern when your intuition is trying to tell you something versus what you think is "logical thought," that is actually just clouding your judgment. **Listen to and trust your instincts**! It's time to focus on hearing and listening to the inner you that has been ignored for so long. Spend time in and with nature. Meditate daily. Practice a little yoga on a regular basis. Get a coach to show you how to go within and listen to your 'Higher Self'. No matter how you choose to do it, reconnect with you and make yourself a priority. Your intuition will once again be remembered and now strengthened. And it's a powerful and truthful force that will never stear you wrong if you choose to follow its wisdom.

If you think there's something wrong there probably is. If you suspect your "**catch**" is being economical with the truth, you have a right to investigate. If there is no issue, the communication skills you develop could bring you both closer as you discover each other's vulnerabilities and work through them together. Conflicts in relationships after all, are one of the most powerful ways to strengthen bonds and intimacy, IF they are handled properly. But that topic is for another book. Keep in mind— *you don't get what you want in life, you get what you are*. So, if you're suspicious because YOU are sneaky or because YOU have something to hide (*people who have nothing to hide, hide nothing*) <u>YOU</u> are the one psychologically projecting the lack of trust and unhealthiness onto your partner and YOU need to take a step back and embark on some self reflection. If that is not the case and you've got a *THROW BACK*, then brace yourself for the release.

Case in point, you might find you have a hybrid *THROW BACK*. Such as, a *Barra-Leech*, *Gefilte-Dog*, *Shar-anha*, *Octo-cuda*, *Gold-Dog*, *Jelly-cuda*, *Piranha-pus*, and *Fire-Jelly*, etc. The possibilities are endless! You might even find a *THROW BACK* who demonstrates the behaviors or attitudes of multiple (or God forbid – ALL) the *THROW BACK*s. Listen to your instincts!! If your instincts are warning you to "*THROW BACK*," then TRUST THEM and take action. If he's not a *THROW BACK* you'll discover that, but if he is… he's already out to sea.

2. KNOW YOURSELF AND GROW YOURSELF

No matter your endeavor, it is CRITICAL to not only know yourself but be willing to grow and expand as a human being and as a partner. You need to know who you are and what you stand for, and you need to know your physical- and emotional- self. Beyond that, every single person needs to be willing to grow and expand throughout their relationships. Here is an interesting fact to ponder: everything in the Universe is either growing or dying. That means the flowers, humans, trees, animals, YOU and yes, your relationship is either growing or it's dying. So if you feel stuck or stagnant in your partnership that means it's dying. It's not expanding. No human being stops growing in some way from birth until death. Yet we've developed this insane way of handling our relationships that involves "finding the one", then doing nothing more to grow, cultivate, nourish, or expand who you are, who your partner is, and what your relationship is. This is nuts! So basically, once married, you stop trying and just exist next to a person who is also just existing. That is a recipe for failure. And even if you actually stay together "forever", the passion will die out, and the emotional, mental, physical, and eventually the sexual, intimacy will fade. Why? Because if you're not growing you're dying. That's the law of every living thing in the universe.

How many relationship courses from experts have you taken? How many online seminars have you and your partner attended together? How many of you have ever even heard of the six basic needs according to human needs psychology and how to lovingly and selflessly meet them for your partner? If you're reading magazines to get relationship advice and to find out how to ignite passion back into your relationships, then you're fooling yourself. Learning what it really means to nurture and grow a healthy, passionate relationship or how to revive a broken one takes expert teaching and coaching from a highly qualified person. We have all learned to wait until crisis mode or when close to divorce before seeking out help, and that's if you're even willing to get help. Think about it. If you don't spend time on your education, or on training to acquire a skill set, then how are you qualified to be the engineer, mechanic, professor, business owner, physical or occupational therapist, or to hold ANY job title at all? You can't even work a job as a high school student without on-the -job training. Yet, when it comes to relationships, nothing. We don't learn it in school and it is not encouraged by our culture to strengthen your relationship and love skills before diving in. Therefore, you start engaging in something that you have absolutely no clue how to do in a healthy and loving way, make a million mistakes, get your heart broken once or twenty times, and then blame relationships or other people for your aching heart and bitterness.

Ugh. People. . . its time to stop the madness. It's time to put your own, personal growth at the top of the list of life's priorities and learn from the very best you can find to teach you the skills and tools you need to cultivate a loving, magnificent and everlasting relationship. It's not hard once you know how and you gain the skill set! Look at society's results! If people already knew how to do this, the divorce and infidelity rates wouldn't be so astronomical.

It's key to learn about the inner you and what subconscious beliefs and behavioral patterns you hold that create the dating and relationship experiences you've had up to this point. Most people are clueless about the patterns they run so they simply blame their ex for the bad experience. Every person has blind spots: ways of behaving that are so automatic you aren't even aware that you do certain things. These reactions to people and circumstances create your relationship experiences. Have you ever had an argument with a significant other and you have no idea what the hell the other person is even mad about? They, or you, are functioning from their blind spots. This is why it's so important to learn and grow when it comes to love and relationships. You need to understand all four of your bodies: the mental, emotional, physical, and spiritual and how they function when connected to another person.

Your spiritual body is what holds your intuition. Your mental and emotional reactions to people and circumstances stem from your life experiences thus far; culture, upbringing, and family and social influences. And your physical body needs to be understood and listened to as well.

You need to know your *physical* self and take charge of your body! It is your temple and you are its keeper. When it comes to your sexual self, know where you like to be touched and how. You don't need *someone else* to climax, remember! A vibrator can be your BFF! Sex has mental, emotional and physical components and the more in tune you are with yourself the better all of your relationships will be. One thing to keep in mind, "If you masturbate you're guaranteed an orgasm WITHOUT the risk of STDs or pregnancy."

Take charge of YOUR body and YOUR orgasms. If you are with somebody, an all important take home message is that **all women have a right to orgasm too**! Yeah, you read that right. Why is it that women are the ones who naturally have the ability to achieve multiple orgasms, but often don't even have ONE?! I personally think for every guy's one orgasm the woman that he is with should have three! Why in the world do women settle for sub-par sex when the guy they're with "finishes" every time they have sex? Guys, if you were right in the middle of having sex, your partner had an orgasm, and then simply stopped all sexual activity with you in that moment, how frustrating do you think it would be?! Especially if it occurred the majority of the time you had sex together!! Don't you think that would get old really fast? You would be less and less likely to continue having sex with her if it was *that* dissatisfying. So, HELLO to all men out there who have a selfish sexual appetite and don't take the time or make the effort to please their partner. You will be more likely to get sex from your lover more often if she knows it will be pleasurable for her too. This isn't rocket science! If two partners are engaging in a sexual relationship, then BOTH partners are entitled to be satisfied. If one partner continues to get "snuffed" during sexual encounters together, wouldn't it make sense that sex would become increasingly *less* enticing? This is such SELFISH behavior and it has a negative impact on every aspect of your partner, (mental and emotional), not just her sexual appetite.

Ladies if you're partner isn't making the effort to satisfy you sexually, then some ideas of possibly throwing him back should be swimming around in your head. His actions, or lack thereof, show a selfish side and that he doesn't care enough about you to please you. Now don't get me wrong, it can be challenging for a man to please a woman. And ladies, it is your responsibility to communicate with your partner to let him know what your needs are in the sack. Guide him and instruct him. Tell him what pleases you. It should be important to him to pleasure you, but it's just as important for you to show him how you want to be pleasured in order to achieve an orgasm. However, if you've tried to communicate your sexual needs and he just doesn't seem to value your equal right to sexual gratification, then you should know by now what to do. THROW. . .HIM. . .BACK . . .and find a better **catch** who values you, not only as a person, but as a sexual being.

3. SET HEALTHY BOUNDARIES AND LIMITATIONS

When you know yourself and trust your instincts, it is much easier to maintain healthy boundaries. If you can maintain your own boundaries; you can aid/support/assist others as well. You won't be interested in someone else's **catch** and won't tolerate negative behavior towards you or anyone else. You'll inherently remember to SIGN OFF, you'll abide by TAKEN = TAKEN, and you'll stand up for your sisters. You won't degrade yourself by fighting over a **catch** or a person who is emotionally unavailable, or over someone who demonstrates the characteristics of a *THROW BACK*. You'll take your time before having sex. And if you've forgotten what counts as "sex" review the chapter on *MINNOWS*. By making someone show patience for sex you'll discover VERY QUICKLY what that person's true intentions are. This is a good thing because it clears the path for your **Big Tuna / Angel Fish**.

What if you're NOT looking for anything serious? Be HONEST, be DIRECT, and be SAFE. Always communicate your intentions because other people have a RIGHT to decide how to interact with you based on FACTUAL information. Even if you are looking for a fling, you STILL need to act with self-respect and dignity, and in consideration of others, because no matter your intentions, you still need to SIGN OFF. You must refrain from fighting over a **catch**, and must always remember that TAKEN = TAKEN. Also, if someone tells you they aren't interested in a relationship – BELIEVE THEM. You're fooling yourself if your narrative is that they'll change their minds while their narrative is that they do not want a relationship. Committing to someone who has been direct about not wanting a relationship and pretending that you're ok with that when you're not only closes you off to meeting someone who IS in the same internal space as you. And it sets you up to become angry and resentful.

Let's also point something out that most people carry in their blind spots. Sleeping around means you are literally USING people for your own selfish, sexual gratification. There is nothing selfless about one-night stands and promiscuity. Your goal is to use someone as a sexual object so you can orgasm. When you use people for sex it makes you nothing more than a superficial, selfish user. In other words, you are a *THROW BACK*. Now, no one is judging. But we are calling it what it is. There is no amount of superficial sexual pleasure that comes close to the sexual pleasure one can achieve from a deeply intimate relationship where both parties are selflessly devoted to their partner's pleasure. When a relationship is dying vs. growing, the sex always diminishes or even stops. After going through coaching, couples have reported that their newfound sexal intimacy was a million times better and more pleasureable than when they were even first dating. It always blows people's minds that something that they've done so many times before, suddenly has a new passion and a new pleasure threshold. Those that pursue how to improve their sex lives, but never put the effort into improving themselves and the emotional and mental intimacy first, will never achieve the highest levels of sexual pleasure that exist. The deepest levels of sexual pleasure only exist through a bonding with and nurturing of your partner's spiritual, mental, emotional, and physical bodies. Note: physical body doesn't mean sexual body.

What's the bottom line? Take responsibility for your actions – YOU HAVE CHOICES. Continuing to be selfish and reckless is not only destructive to others; it's also destructive to you. You can't harm others without also harming yourself in the long run. You will suffer the consequences AND reap the benefits of your decisions, but it all comes down to you *owning* that you are in charge of your life and the shape it takes.

4. FOUR SEASONS

Finally, real relationships take effort and it takes time to get to know someone. Our personal belief is it takes a minimum of four seasons. Four seasons is about the right amount of time to have made intellectual, emotional, and romantic connections with an individual. This leads to the "seeing what happens" stage and/or the "falling in love" stage (with all the expectations and responsibilities that come with those phases), and in about four seasons you're likely to have been in enough of a range of situations with your partner that will help you really get to know each other. Creating a successful, healthy relationship is a process. It takes time to get to know each other through a variety of circumstances and situations. Sharing adventures, personal space, secrets, laughter, and experiences only build intimacy and the bond between the couple. It takes time to build those experiences. It's also important to understand this process is never-ending. If the couple is able to communicate effectively, accommodate one another, and is willing to be vulnerable to each other's needs, the couple has THE RECIPE for a rewarding long-term partnership. Such a relationship cannot be cultivated over night, and this process truly should be unfolding forever. However, at least use the "four seasons" approach to facilitate the process and help you choose the partner that's right for you.

What's most important to understand is that having fun experiences is NO indicator if you two are "meant to be" or not. Anyone can have a great time given fun circumstances. It's not the fun times that determine longevity, but the bad times. When conflicts arise, How do you come together and work as a team to support one another? Or- does conflict turn into a rift between you both that creates distance, a lack of trust, and resentment? If that starts to happen, you need to seek help immediately. How you handle conflict is one of the biggest factors that determines if a couple stays together or not, and is *the key factor* in building and maintaining trust. Conflicts are beautiful opportunities to deepen your relationship. But if you view them as negative and just fight when something challenging arises, that means you lack vital and necessary skills required to create lasting, harmonious love. And you better seek out help and gain those skills ASAP. Otherwise you'll watch yet another potential **catch** swim away from you.

5. HOW YOU'LL KNOW...

How will you know when you're with your BIG TUNA or your ANGEL FISH?

☐ Your instincts tell you you are.

☐ You make decisions together as a team.

☐ Conflicts are resolved together with loving support vs. fighting.

☐ You love him/her "through their ugly". You support and nurture each other but never enable.

☐ You are right by each other's side during hard times.

☐ There is no "keeping score". You love doing selfless things simply because it makeshim/her smile and s/he does the same for you.

☐ You each can draw healthy boundaries and they are respected by the other.

☐ You both make a commitment to learning, growing, & enhancing your relationship so it doesn't get stale and die.

☐ You each choose forgiveness instead of resentment.

☐ You trust each other.

☐ You feel like you're a better person by being with him/her.

☐ S/he inspires you to grow and be the best version of you that you can be.

☐ Each of your dreams are supported and nourished by the other.

☐ You each enjoy doing selfless things for the other person, asking nothing in return.

☐ You don't *need* him/her, but instead choose him/her.

☐ You find out what makes the other feel loved and then you offer that to each other.

☐ You each think in terms of WE instead of ME.

☐ You put each other first. That means before friends and family! (This is of course when you are seriously committed to one another.

S/he needs to earn the right to be put first). And no, it doesn't mean you forget about other people you care about.

☐ You each engage in the relationship with honesty, open communication, and transparency.

☐ Neither one of you wears a mask. You show your true selves to the other.

☐ You are FAITHFUL to each other…no exceptions.

☐ He never sent you an unsolicited dick pic!

In summary, you show love and respect for yourself and for the other person. You share a common core purpose and each helps the other to be a better person. You support each other through the lows and help each other reach new heights, because you both deal with frustration, disappointment, and setbacks in healthy ways. And if you don't know how to deal with conflicts and life challenges in healthy, stress free ways, *you're willing to learn and you actively seek out the help to gain these skills.*

You feel good around the other person because they help you feel even better about who you are. You provide a safe haven for each other emotionally and spiritually and this support not only brings you closer, but also brings joy into your life.

You *listen* to one another, with the goal of connecting and understanding, NOT with the intent to rebut, prove the other wrong, or make yourself right.

You both value and nurture your primary relationship. Your relationship with each other is central and you not only cherish it, but you guard and protect it.

You trust the other and yourself to *never* make unilateral decisions because there is an inherent understanding that your life is intertwined, and joint decisions are imperative to a healthy and happy partnership. Unilateral decision-making destroys trust and devalues the other person.

You are positive, healthy influences on one another and you can rely on the other to enhance your life, rather than diminish it, as you have a strong, moral and ethical compass that guides all you do together and apart.

In essence, you've found a person secure in his/her skin, who is well adjusted, knows what is important in this life, gives you both a safe place to be and grow, and is willing to walk that path with you. Such a place is where all levels of intimacy and health grow, and where people THRIVE! Anything less is a *THROW BACK!*

Look, no one is perfect. A **Big Tuna** or an **Angel Fish** didn't become that way through perfection. That doesn't exist. Everyone has accumulated unhealthy behavior patterns that need to be realized and changed in order to cultivate a healthy, loving, passionate, and ever-lasting relationship. The point is, a **Big Tuna** or an **Angel Fish** already knows this and is doing the work (or already has done this work) on themselves. They've emotionally matured enough to make self-awareness and self-growth a priority. Being able to snag your greatest catch means you first become another's greatest catch, which means you develop, you strengthen, you emotionally mature, and you expand YOURSELF! Snagging your greatest catch doesn't happen without the willingness and devotion to becoming YOUR best self. It's never too late to do so. It's always just one choice away.

6. SHARE YOUR FISH TALE! AND HELP EMPOWER OTHERS...

Have you met your **Big Tuna** or your *ANGEL FISH*? Are you with a *THROW BACK?* Are your friends *BLOWFISH?* Do you have some *THROW BACK* tales to tell? What's your story? Do you have a fish profile we've not covered here that you would like to share with us? We invite you to share your tales on our facebook page: https://www.facebook.com/findingacatch/

ABOUT THE AUTHORS

RACHEL FIORI is an Ascension Coach (elevating your life and relationships to new heights), Energy Healer, & Psychic. She has her Masters of Science degree in Occupational Therapy, and has also earned her certification as a Strategic Intervention Life Coach. Rachel uses her profound psychic, healing gifts and expertise to transform people's lives and their relationships. Rachel provides seminars, workshops, and coaching to unblock the barriers in people's lives and relationships that lead them to their purpose, fulfillment, success, and unconditional love. Rachel resides in San Diego, CA and coaches and heals people throughout the United States and internationally.

If you are interested in a seminar, workshop, or receiving relationship or life coaching you can contact Rachel through her website: www.fiorilifetransformation.com or email her directly at: fiorilifetransformation@gmail.com.

MELISSA FIORI is a tenured Associate professor of Second Language Acquisition and Applied Linguistics (Ph.D. from Penn State) at a small private college in upstate New York, who studied Literature, Language & Culture of the Spanish-speaking world at Middlebury College (M.A.) and International Relations & Spanish at Bucknell University (B.A.). She has published her research in peer-reviewed journals, such as CALICO and ITDL and is an alumna of the Woodhull Institute for Ethical Leadership for Women.

GLOSSARY

Angel Fish: The female equivalent of the **Big Tuna**. A true **catch**, kind, compassionate, intelligent and beautiful from the inside out!

ANGLERFISH: The Sugar Baby.

Bar Jack: Drinks like a fish, lives by the motto, "It's 5:00 somewhere."

Barracuda: Relies on *lie-in-wait* tactics to prey on girls in vulnerable states.

BIG TUNA: He's what we're all looking for! He's our big **catch**!

Blowfish: The female equivalent of a *THROW BACK*, they tolerate disrespectful behaviors and lack integrity.

Catfish: Predators who pretend to be someone or something they're not with the intention of using and abusing their target, usually through online social networks.

Dogfish: They typically have egos the size of Great Whites, they're devious, conniving schemers who over populate our waters.

Firemouth: The mental, physical, psychological abuser.

Flounder: Flip – floppers, they can either flip themselves into **Big Tuna** status OR they can flop onto the side of the *THROW BACK*.

Gefilte: Loves & accepts you, only if you're the same culture/religion or converts to his religion.

Gold Fish: Kings of bling.

Guppy: Small-towners who sometimes suffer from *big fish small pond syndrome*.

Jellyfish: The spineless Mama's Boy!

Leech: Parasite that will suck you dry of anything it can get its bloodsucking jaws around.

Minnows: Impressionable teens who can be guided to become respectable fish, or misguided into adopting *THROW BACK* behavior.

Octopus: Mr. Grabby Hands. Skeevy little creatures who don't know how to respect personal boundaries.

Penis Fish: The STD fish! Be in the know when it comes to Sexually Transmitted Diseases.

Pilot Fish: Side-kicks of *THROW BACK*s and other more dominant fish.

Piranha: Predatory fish whose behavior is worse in schools, watch out for Frat boys because they often fall into this category.

Puffer Fish: The pothead.

Rainbow Fish: The closet gay.

Shark: Emotionally unavailable predators; top of the food chain; wears a self-proclaimed **Big Tuna** mask to lure you in.

Slippery Dick: The cheater, his penis slides into places it just shouldn't go.

Sucker Fish: Make excuses for Throw Backs and refuse to cut the line

FISH IDIOMS

A big fish: an important and/or powerful person.

A big fish in a small pond: an important and/or powerful person who would have much less clout if part of a larger group/organization/institution.

Clam up: to fall silent, refuse to talk or to stop talking.

A cold fish: unfriendly, a person who does not show emotions or is not very sociable.

Another/ a different kettle of fish:

When some one/thing is a different kettle of fish, it means he/she/it is totally different from some one/thing else that has been spoken about.

Drink like a fish: drinks copious amounts of alcohol, frequently.

A fine kettle of fish: a mess, a difficult situation.

A fish out of water: uncomfortable, awkward, or unfamiliar with a situation.

Fish for compliments: a person who looks for praise and tries to get people to say nice things about him/her.

Fish for (something): to try to get information on or about someone/thing.

Fish in troubled waters: to get involved in a difficult/dangerous/confusing situation.

Fish or cut bait: make a decision; said when someone needs to make up his mind without further delay.

Fishy: suspicious, shady, odd, and dubious; *also: smells fishy*.

Green around the gills: to look / feel sick.

Happy as a clam: to be very happy/content.

Have bigger fish to fry: to have more important/interesting things to do, to have other opportunities at your disposal.

Holy Mackeral! Expresses surprise or disbelief.

Like shooting fish in a barrel: mix-matched strengths—unbalanced competition— in which the extreme weakness of the one side is clearly no match for the strength of the other.

Live in a fish bowl: to live in a place where everyone knows one another.

Neither fish nor fowl: some one/thing that is difficult to define, group or categorize because he/she/it has characteristics of two different entities simultaneously.

Not the only fish in the sea: there are other options from which to choose and also: *plenty of fish in the sea.*

Packed in like sardines: crowded.

Plenty of fish in the sea: there are other options from which to choose and also: *not the only fish in the sea.*

Shark: a cruel, callous, heartless, ruthless person who usually lies, deceives and betrays.

Slippery as an eel: not trustworthy

Small fry: unimportant

Swim like a fish: to be a good swimmer.

A whale of a time: to have a great time.

The world is your oyster: the world is at your fingertips; you've got the potential to do great things.

CPSIA information can be obtained
at www.ICGtesting.com
Printed in the USA
LVHW02s2303200818
587601LV00008B/230/P